D0493275

GREENFINGERS GUIDES
EVERGREEN PLANTS

LUCY SUMMERS

headline

Copyright © Hort Couture 2012
Photographs © Garden World Images Ltd
except those listed on p.128

The right of Lucy Summers to be identified as the Author
of the Work has been asserted by her in accordance with
the Copyright, Designs and Patents Act 1988.

First published in 2012
by HEADLINE PUBLISHING GROUP

1

Lucy Summers would be happy to hear from readers
with their comments on the book at the following
e-mail address: lucy@greenfingersguides.co.uk

The Greenfingers Guides series concept was originated
by Lucy Summers and Darley Anderson

Apart from any use permitted under UK copyright law,
this publication may only be reproduced, stored, or
transmitted, in any form, or by any means, with prior
permission in writing of the publishers or, in the case of
reprographic production, in accordance with the terms of
licences issued by the Copyright Licensing Agency.

A CIP catalogue record for this title is available from
the British Library

ISBN 978 0 7553 6121 2

Design by Isobel Gillan
Printed and bound in Italy by Canale & C.S.p.A.

Headline's policy is to use papers that are natural,
renewable and recyclable products and made from wood
grown in sustainable forests. The logging and
manufacturing processes are expected to conform to the
environmental regulations of the country of origin.

HEADLINE PUBLISHING GROUP
An Hachette UK Company
338 Euston Road
London NW1 3BH

www.headline.co.uk
www.hachette.co.uk
www.greenfingersguides.co.uk
www.theopengardencompany.co.uk
www.lovelucysummers.com

LONDON BOROUGH OF HACKNEY LIBRARIES	
HK11000613	
Bertrams	21/03/2012
635.97	£12.99
	15/03/2012

DEDICATION
Thanks M & E for all your constant plodding beside me.
And to Serena, without whom these books would not be
nearly as good as they are.

OTHER TITLES IN THE GREENFINGERS GUIDES SERIES:

Drought-Tolerant Plants
ISBN 978 0 7553 1759 2

Fruit and Vegetables
ISBN 978 0 7553 1761 5

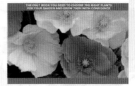

Climbers and Wall Shrubs
ISBN 978 0 7553 1758 5

Border Flowers
ISBN 978 0 7553 1760 8

Fragrant Plants
ISBN 978 0 7553 6120 5

Contents

Introduction

One of my earliest recollections is of a secret garden. It was hidden behind the shrubbery at school, through an archway cut into a very tall hedge. In the deep charcoal shadows of the hedge the opening appeared black, and the moment you stepped from dappled sunlight into the cool, damp, mossy sanctuary of the secret garden, you felt you had entered a mystical kingdom. We were banned from this area, which made it all the more alluring, and we were convinced it was inhabited by trolls and ogres.

Here was a garden of giant topiary sculptures that loomed ominously above, casting their shadows across a lawn that resembled black ice. A rectangular pond in the centre was full of dark water that lay as still as sleep. We would tuck ourselves into the hedge's chill caves (really alcoves that had been cut into the yew) and dare each other to run across, dip our hands into the water and dash back. The idea was to avoid getting caught by the demon who lurked under the water, waiting to drag us down into his fearful watery domain. The topiary figures who reigned in this shady bower seemed to glide like figures on a chessboard and we swore they moved every time we turned our backs. There was not a flower in that garden, as I recall. Everything was sculpted with loving precision into deep, cooling, green layers that filled the space like textured velvet.

I have since been back to visit this mysterious oasis of childhood and of course it is smaller than I remembered. But the long shadows remain and the air is one of peaceful tranquillity, with every green in nature's palette represented, tinted to shades of black, with the sun eternally shunned by the evergreen ramparts. Without a perennial to lift the composition, this garden is an elegant, serene room born of imagination, diversion, tonal colours and shapes; it remains a living, breathing sanctuary of calm.

As a young gardener I avoided evergreen plants like the plague, so distracted was I by the endless species and varieties of showy perennials. But all gardeners' tastes mature and change, rather like throwing out the chintz and Victoriana and updating with modern fabrics and furniture. With experience, I learnt that a garden without evergreen scaffolding is destined for ordinariness.

In my thirties I became (and still remain) an ardent fan of good old dependable shrubs, though trees and perennials complete the circle. I spent two glorious summers on an orgy of tree and shrub-planting, following the old adage, 'Plant a tree under whose shade you never expect to sit.' It was absolute heaven. Though indisputably indulgent, planting for posterity is very satisfying. There is nothing like leaving something beautiful on the planet for future generations to enjoy.

OPPOSITE Tall hedges and topiary give form and shape to a formal evergreen garden

Choosing evergreen plants

Welcome to the intriguing world of evergreen plants. If you think this book is going to be all about hedges and conifers, think again. Evergreens can certainly form the backbone of gardens, with their richly textured foliage which lasts all year round, but they also include a wonderful array of beautiful flowering perennials and climbers as well as the more familiar shrubs and trees. Some evergreens make diminutive carpets of foliage and flower, while others grow into handsome specimens that offer heirloom planting for generations to come.

Over the centuries, every landscaper worth his salt has relied on elegant evergreen bones to create gardens of lasting beauty. Evergreens are quietly dependable work-horses, and provide an invaluable source of background form and colour every day of the year. Unlike the more short-lived herbaceous perennials, most give many decades of service, doing their thing discreetly, with restrained elegance and minimum fanfare.

Although evergreen plants keep their leaves all year round, they do still suffer leaf loss (you only have to look under a holly bush to see the dry, brown, crackled fallen leaves). However, this is hardly noticeable because of the abundance of constantly renewed growth. Semi-evergreen plants are more likely to drop their leaves in severe winters but by and large they hang on to them in milder years.

There are some plants that are technically semi-evergreen but look a little battered in winter or aren't large enough to add significant interest during the winter months. These include dianthus and some lovely semi-evergreen grasses and climbers,

BELOW Pampas grass (*Cortaderia selloana*) makes a striking focal point

such as the gorgeous *Akebia quinata*; I have deliberately left them out of this book. There was also no room for plants such as *Ribes speciosum*, whose new leaves appear as the old ones die off in winter, but which is not strictly evergreen.

The lovely helianthemums also had to go because, while some are reliably evergreen and the flowers are undeniably wonderful, their foliage is not so striking that you would grow them for leaf interest alone. However, I have included some of the silver-leaved plants, such as lavender and *Convolvulus cneorum*. Although these are certainly better looking in summer, they do add an unmistakable grey-silver mass to the borders in winter.

In this book you will find a surprising variety of evergreen plants that you may never have considered using in your garden, simply because it is not widely understood that there is more to evergreen planting than growing hedges. Evergreens are every bit as interesting, versatile and diverse as deciduous garden plants and you get to enjoy the pleasure of their company all year round. Once you turn the last page I hope you will have become an ardent convert, wondering how you ever got along without them. Have fun.

Using this book

Each plant listed is categorised according to season and its eventual height (all measurements are approximate), with useful, practical cultivation advice that will encourage you to grow with ever-greater enjoyment, creativity and confidence. More detailed information, covering all the different elements mentioned in the profiles, and including help with planting and propagation, will be found after the plant profiles. Lists of plants for specific purposes can be found at the back of the book.

Throughout the book, plants are arranged seasonally, but in practice the corresponding months will vary according to local weather patterns, regional differences and the effects of climate change. Additionally, the flowering times of many plants span more than one season. The seasons given are based in the British Isles,

and should be thought of as a flexible guide.

Latin names have been given for all the plants in this book because these are the names that are universally used when describing plants; the Latin name should be recognised by the garden centre, and with any luck you will be sold the right plant. Common names have also been given, but these vary from country to country, and even within a country, and a plant may not be recognised by its common name.

Skill level is indicated by one of three ratings: **EASY**, **MEDIUM** or **TRICKY**

Many of the plants chosen for this book have been given the Award of Garden Merit (AGM) by the Royal Horticultural Society (RHS). This is a really useful pointer in helping you decide which plants to buy. The AGM is intended to be of practical value to the ordinary gardener, and plants that merit the award are the cream of the crop. The RHS is continually assessing new plant cultivars and you can be sure that any plant with an AGM will have excellent decorative features and be:

- easily available to the buying public
- easy to grow and care for
- not particularly susceptible to pests or disease
- robust and healthy

Early spring	March	Early autumn	September
Mid-spring	April	Mid-autumn	October
Late spring	May	Late autumn	November
Early summer	June	Early winter	December
Mid-summer	July	Mid-winter	January
Late summer	August	Late winter	February

SPRING

Spring marks the start of the growing season but evergreen plants are already streets ahead of the game. While herbaceous plants are only just beginning to stir into new growth, the evergreens have been flaunting their foliage and berries through the autumn and winter months.

You might be forgiven for thinking that the dependable old evergreens would have reached exhaustion point by now. Think again. As if they haven't already performed admirably enough, many evergreens still have beautiful, often fragrant, flowers to offer in spring, to rival and complement existing garden plants, as well as encouraging wildlife, nesting birds and nectar-seeking butterflies into your outdoor spaces.

Ajuga reptans 'Burgundy Glow'

Bugle

↑ 15cm/6in ↔ 60–90cm/24–36in **EASY**

Widely found from Asia to Europe, this handy little plant is an unfussy, rapidly spreading, rhizomatous evergreen perennial. It creeps steadily across the ground, making excellent ground cover. Handsome oval green leaves (8cm/3in long) are splashed with vivid silver and burgundy marbling, and the flower spires are small but perfectly painted, with rich bright blue whorled flowers contrasting with pale lilac and white lipped flags. *A.r.* 'Catlin's Giant' has larger bronze leaves; *A.r.* 'Multicolor' has burgundy, cream and pink marbled leaves.

BEST USES Excellent ground cover in shady corners, under trees or on awkward banks and slopes; pretty in spring borders and cottage gardens

FLOWERS April to May
SCENTED No
ASPECT North, east or west facing, in a sheltered position; partial to full shade (flowers fade when planted in full sun)
SOIL Any fertile, moist, well-drained soil
HARDINESS Fully hardy at temperatures down to -15°C/5°F; needs no winter protection
DROUGHT TOLERANCE Excellent, once established
PROBLEMS Powdery mildew
CARE Remove spent flower heads to keep plants tidy; dig up unwanted spread
PROPAGATION Division in spring; detach and pot up rooted plantlets in spring or autumn; softwood cuttings in early summer

Andromeda polifolia 'Compacta'
Bog rosemary

⬆ 30cm/12in ⬌ 30cm/12in　　　　　EASY

Originally found growing wild in Japan, this fairly slow-growing, spreading, mounding evergreen perennial has colonised easily in northern Europe. The tough, narrow, linear, blue-green leaves (3cm/1¼in long), with white under-sides, resemble rosemary foliage and form thick, slightly domed matting. Generous dangling clusters of tiny, spherical, pale pinky white flower buds hang prettily from short stems and open to small, belled flowers (3cm/1¼in across) that last for weeks on end in spring. *A.p.* 'Nikko' has soft pink flowers; *A.p.* 'Blue Ice' has steely blue flowers.

> **BEST USES** Ideal ground cover in woodland or peaty soils; suits damp (not waterlogged), shady beds; does well in pots, with ericaceous compost

FLOWERS April to June
SCENTED No
ASPECT Any, in a sheltered position; full sun to partial shade
SOIL Any fertile, moist, well-drained acid soil
HARDINESS Fully hardy at temperatures down to -15°C/5°F; needs no winter protection
DROUGHT TOLERANCE Poor
PROBLEMS None
CARE Trim lightly from mid- to late spring, for tidiness
PROPAGATION Layering in spring or autumn; detach and pot up rooted plantlets in spring or autumn; softwood cuttings in early to mid-summer

Arabis alpina subsp. *caucasica* 'Schneehaube'

⬆ 5cm/2in ⬌ 45cm/18in　　　　　EASY

This energetic southern European evergreen perennial makes carpets of small, spooned, slightly toothed grey-green leaves (5cm/2in long) that form leafy rosettes which perk up quickly after a long winter. In spring, it is smothered in small, single, shallow, star-shaped four-petalled white flowers (1cm/³⁄₈in across), which give the charming effect of settled snow or a foaming gush of flowing water. *A.a.* subsp. *c.* 'Flore Pleno' has pure white double flowers.

> **BEST USES** Ideal for the rock, alpine, gravel or Mediterranean garden; makes good ground cover in a hot sunny spot and on poor, stony slopes and banks; grows well in containers and pots

FLOWERS May to June
SCENTED No
ASPECT Any, in a sheltered or exposed position; full sun
SOIL Any fertile, well-drained soil
HARDINESS Fully hardy at temperatures down to -15°C/5°F; needs no winter protection
DROUGHT TOLERANCE Excellent, once established
PROBLEMS Can be invasive
CARE Deadhead or trim lightly after flowering, for tidiness and to prevent self-seeding; has a tendency to exceed its allotted space, so pull up any unwanted spread
PROPAGATION Softwood cuttings in summer; sow seed in pots in a cold frame in autumn

Arenaria montana 🏆
Sandwort

⬆ 5cm/2in ⬌ 30cm/12in   **EASY**

Hailing from the mountains of south-west Europe, this energetic evergreen perennial makes a dense, thick carpet in no time. It has small, narrow, linear deep grey-green leaves (2cm/¾in long). In summer, short, smooth, slender stems are topped with small, simple, star-shaped pure snow white flowers (roughly the same size as the leaves) which are lightly veined and have light yellow-green centres. This is an unfussy, low-maintenance plant that is ideal for the beginner and those difficult dry, sunny spots with poor soil.

> **BEST USES** Ideal for banks of builders' rubble, awkward slopes, rockeries, gravel and Mediterranean gardens or hot sunny borders; great between paving and edging in borders; easy in pots

FLOWERS May to June

SCENTED No

ASPECT Any, in a sheltered or exposed position; full sun

SOIL Any fertile, well-drained soil

HARDINESS Fully hardy at temperatures down to -15°C/5°F; needs no winter protection

DROUGHT TOLERANCE Excellent, once established

PROBLEMS None

CARE Deadhead after flowering to maintain dense foliage growth

PROPAGATION Division in spring; sow seed in pots in a cold frame in autumn

Armeria juniperifolia 'Bevan's Variety' 🏆
Thrift

⬆ 5cm/2in ⬌ 15cm/6in   **EASY**

This charming evergreen alpine shrublet originates from the craggy mountain areas of southern Spain and is easy to grow, thriving quite contentedly in poor soil. Thrift commonly ranges in colour from whites to pinky purples, some of which can be a bit wishy-washy. This variety has typical thrift-like narrow, linear, grass-like green leaves (1.5cm/½in long) that form tight, neat little cushions of evergreen foliage. Come spring, short, slender, wiry stems are topped with pretty, rounded, double, deep rosy pink flowers. *A.j.* 'Alba' has white flowers.

> **BEST USES** Ideal as a low-maintenance plant for the rock, alpine or gravel and Mediterranean garden; makes good ground cover planted in numbers in a hot sunny spot or on poor, stony slopes and banks; easy in containers and pots

FLOWERS March to May

SCENTED No

ASPECT Any, in a sheltered or exposed position; full sun

SOIL Any fertile, well-drained soil

HARDINESS Fully hardy at temperatures down to -15°C/5°F; needs no winter protection

DROUGHT TOLERANCE Excellent, once established

PROBLEMS None

CARE Deadhead after flowering to prevent self-seeding

PROPAGATION Division in spring; sow seed in pots in a cold frame in spring or autumn; semi-ripe cuttings in summer

Asarum hartwegii
Wild ginger

⬆ 5cm/2in ↔ 30cm/12in   MEDIUM

This low-lying evergreen perennial from the woodlands of the USA has very handsome, vein-etched, polished, deep green kidney-shaped leaves (13cm/5in long), marbled grey. Held on wiry, bristly, plum-coloured stems, the tubular flowers (5cm/2in long) are puce-brown, opening to reveal tri-lobed deep maroon-brown petals edged in cream, with creamy rays radiating from the yellow-green centres.

BEST USES Perfect ground cover for humus-rich woodland areas or shady, gloomy corners of the garden; does well in pots and containers

FLOWERS April to June

SCENTED Aromatic leaves

ASPECT Any, in a sheltered or exposed position; partial to full shade

SOIL Any fertile, well-drained soil

HARDINESS Fully hardy at temperatures down to -15°C/5°F; needs no winter protection

DROUGHT TOLERANCE Poor

PROBLEMS Slugs and snails

CARE Deadhead after flowering to maintain dense foliage growth; if growing in pots, water from the base, avoiding splashing the leaves

PROPAGATION Division in early spring; sow ripe seed immediately in pots in a cold frame

GREENFINGER TIP *This can be slow to establish, but with humus-rich soil (slight acidity will prove a bonus, though is not essential) it will form a green carpet before long*

Aubrieta 'Argenteovariegata' ⚜

⬆ 5cm/2in ↔ Indefinite   EASY

Originating from Asia and Europe, this low-growing evergreen perennial has tiny, roundly oval mid-green leaves, edged in creamy silver, which make pleasing pillows and tumble down walls and banks. In spring an absolute frenzy of small, single, four-petalled pinky purple flowers (1.5cm/½in across) obscure the greenery completely; it retains its tidy foliage through winter. There are many varieties, in shades of pink, purple, mauve or violet. I absolutely adore this for its unfussy, get-on-with-it temperament.

BEST USES Fabulous in rockeries, spilling over old stone walls or softening newly built brick walls; great as ground cover; ideal in pots

FLOWERS March to May

SCENTED No

ASPECT Any, in a sheltered or exposed position; full sun

SOIL Any fertile, well-drained soil

HARDINESS Fully hardy at temperatures down to -15°C/5°F; needs no winter protection

DROUGHT TOLERANCE Good, once established

PROBLEMS Aphids, eelworms and flea beetles; white blister

CARE Trim lightly after flowering to keep the foliage compact and dense

PROPAGATION Sow seed in pots in a cold frame in spring or autumn; semi-ripe cuttings in summer; division in autumn

Carex oshimensis 'Evergold' ⚜
Sedge

⬆ 30cm/12in ⬌ 35cm/14in   **EASY**

This rhizomatous evergreen perennial from Asia forms fountaining mounds of gracefully arching, linear, deep green leaves (25cm/10in long), with creamy yellow striping down the centre of each leaf. Appealing buff-brown grass panicles (3cm/1¼in long) shimmer prettily enough in spring, but it is really grown for its foliage, affording good shape all year long. It is found in damp or soggy ground, in woodland or by water.

BEST USES Grasses suit any modern or urban planting scheme; elegant in formal beds and borders or as ground cover in shady places and woodland; ideal waterside planting; good in pots and containers

FLOWERS April to May; grown mainly for foliage
SCENTED No
ASPECT South, west or east facing, in a sheltered position; full sun to partial shade
SOIL Any fertile, well-drained soil
HARDINESS Fully hardy at temperatures down to -15°C/5°F; needs no winter protection
DROUGHT TOLERANCE Poor
PROBLEMS Aphids, mealybugs and scale insect
CARE Remove any dead or tatty foliage as and when needed
PROPAGATION Division in spring to summer; sow seed in pots in a cold frame in autumn

Cassiope 'Edinburgh' ⚜

⬆ 25cm/10in ⬌ 25cm/10in   **EASY**

These ericaceous (acid-loving) ground-hugging evergreen shrubs come from cold regions of northern America and Europe to the Arctic, and are harsh weather warriors. The wiry, deep green stems are densely packed and covered in overlapping scales of bristly, dark green leaves (8mm/³⁄₈in long). The tiny nodding, snow white flower bells have slightly frilled edges, with distinct brown-maroon calyces prettily clasping the tiny blooms. C. 'Muirhead' ⚜ has white flowers and bushier foliage; C. 'Randle Cook' ⚜ has profuse white flowers.

BEST USES Ideal ground cover in shady woodland or gloomy corners; good for clothing awkward banks and slopes; lovely for rockeries or the front of borders; excellent in pots

FLOWERS May to June
SCENTED No
ASPECT Any, in a sheltered or exposed position; full sun to partial shade
SOIL Any fertile, moist, well-drained acid soil
HARDINESS Fully hardy at temperatures down to -15°C/5°F; needs no winter protection
DROUGHT TOLERANCE Poor
PROBLEMS None
CARE Remove any dead or tatty foliage as needed
PROPAGATION Sow seed in pots in a cold frame in autumn; semi-ripe cuttings in summer

Dryas octopetala
Mountain avens

⬆ 10cm/4in ↔ 90cm/3ft   EASY

This mat-forming alpine evergreen shrublet can be found clinging to rocky ledges, crevices and cliff tops across the northern hemisphere. It has a creeping, carpeting habit, with short, woody stems that bear small, oval, fresh green leaves with crimped edges (4cm/1½in across). From late spring, a fair profusion of shallow, saucer-shaped off-white flowers (4cm/1½in across), with bright golden eyes, stud the foliage and are followed by fluffy seed heads. It is used to a tough, exposed habitat.

BEST USES Perfect in the nooks and crannies of low stone walls or between paving; ideal for ground cover, interplanted with spring bulbs

FLOWERS May to June
SCENTED No
ASPECT South, west or east facing, in a sheltered or exposed position; full sun to partial shade
SOIL Any fertile, humus-rich, gritty, well-drained soil
HARDINESS Fully hardy at temperatures down to -15°C/5°F; needs no winter protection
DROUGHT TOLERANCE Good, once established
PROBLEMS None
CARE Trim lightly after flowering
PROPAGATION Self-seeds easily; detach and pot up rooted plantlets in spring; sow ripe seed immediately in pots in a cold frame; softwood cuttings in summer

Epimedium franchetii
'Brimstone Butterfly'   Barrenwort

⬆ 30cm/12in ↔ 30cm/12in   EASY

This slow-spreading, rhizomatous evergreen perennial has bright green heart-shaped leaves, flushed red when young, from which slender, wiry, upright pale green stems emerge, hung with dainty, nodding, pale yellow lantern-like flowers, with attractive long, spidery, curving lemon-hued spurs. The leaves make thick matting and are burnished copper-bronze in autumn.

BEST USES Reliable ground cover in shade; excellent underplanted with spring bulbs; ideal for awkward slopes or banks; rabbit and deer proof

FLOWERS March to May
SCENTED No
ASPECT North, east or west facing, in a sheltered position with protection from winds; partial shade
SOIL Any fertile, well-drained, humus-rich soil; add leafmould before planting
HARDINESS Fully hardy at temperatures down to -15°C/5°F; needs no winter protection
DROUGHT TOLERANCE Poor
PROBLEMS Vine weevil; late frosts can damage the leaves and flowers
CARE Cut back in late winter/early spring; mulch in winter to protect crowns from frost
PROPAGATION Division after flowering or in autumn; rhizome root cuttings in winter

GREENFINGER TIP *Expect to wait three years for a flowering plant, even from rhizome root cuttings (the best method for epimediums)*

Halimium lasianthum ♉
Woolly rock rose

⬆ 90cm/3ft ⬌ 1.5m/5ft   **EASY**

This low-growing, spreading Mediterranean evergreen shrub looks like the more common rock rose, though the leaves (4cm/1½in long) are smaller and thumbnail-shaped, with a distinctive felty wool covering giving a whitish-grey bloom to the foliage. The shallow, gappy, sunshine yellow flowers (5cm/2in across) are smudged with brown, and make a joyful explosion of brightness from late spring. It should reach mature size within five years and makes an excellent flowering and year-round foliage plant for sunny gardens. *H.l.* 'Concolor' has pure yellow flowers minus the blotches.

BEST USES Excellent ground cover in gravel and Mediterranean gardens; ideal for stony banks; good in sunny borders or in pots on sunny patios

FLOWERS May to June
SCENTED No
ASPECT South or west facing, in a sheltered position; full sun
SOIL Any fertile, well-drained soil
HARDINESS Frost hardy at temperatures down to -5°C/23°F; may need winter protection
DROUGHT TOLERANCE Excellent, once established
PROBLEMS None
CARE Trim lightly in mid- to late spring to maintain size and shape
PROPAGATION Semi-ripe cuttings in late summer

Iberis sempervirens ♉
Candytuft

⬆ 30cm/12in ⬌ 40cm/16in   **EASY**

This ground-hugging evergreen shrublet from the Mediterranean has branching stems of narrow, deep green leaves (3cm/1¼in long) and short, slender stems, smothered in clusters of pure white flowers (5cm/2in across), some of which may be tinged pale lilac, from late spring into early summer. Enduringly popular, it's a reliable, uncomplicated, low-maintenance plant. *I.s.* 'Snowflake' ♉ (15cm/6in tall) is more compact but just as free-flowering.

BEST USES Excellent in rock gardens; good ground cover in gravel and Mediterranean gardens; useful as edging and in sunny borders; ideal for walls, banks and slopes; good in pots, containers and hanging baskets or troughs

FLOWERS May to June
SCENTED No
ASPECT South, west or east facing, in a sheltered position; full sun
SOIL Any fertile, well-drained soil
HARDINESS Fully hardy at temperatures down to -15°C/5°F; needs no winter protection
DROUGHT TOLERANCE Good, once established, in partial shade (not in full sun)
PROBLEMS Slugs and snails; clubroot
CARE Trim lightly after flowering to maintain bushy growth and spread
PROPAGATION Softwood cuttings in late spring; semi-ripe cuttings in spring or summer; sow seed in pots in a cold frame in autumn

Polygala chamaebuxus var. grandiflora
Milkwort/Bastard box

⬆ 15cm/6in ↔ 30cm/12in   **EASY**

I'm not sure that this spreading, evergreen shrub from Europe deserves its common name. Is it a poor man's box? You would hardly think so, looking at its small, tough, handsome, leathery, oval, deep green glossy leaves (2.5cm/1in long). Additionally, from late spring into summer, it bears rather exotic-looking, purple-winged, yellow-tipped, orchid-like waxy-smelling flowers (1.5cm/½in long), which certainly give it the edge over traditional box in the blooming stakes. *P.c.* var. *g.* 'Kamniski' has darker purple flowers.

> **BEST USES** Excellent ground cover in Mediterranean, Japanese, gravel and rock gardens; ideal in pots and containers

FLOWERS May to June
SCENTED Scented flowers
ASPECT South, west or east facing, in a sheltered position; partial to full shade
SOIL Any fertile, moist, well-drained soil
HARDINESS Fully hardy at temperatures down to -15°C/5°F; needs no winter protection
DROUGHT TOLERANCE Good, once established
PROBLEMS None
CARE Low maintenance; remove dead, diseased or damaged wood as needed
PROPAGATION Semi-ripe cuttings in mid- to late summer

Rhododendron 'Azurika'

⬆ 60cm/24in ↔ 80cm/32in   **EASY**

This compact, low-growing evergreen hybrid shrub has small, elliptical, olive green leaves (5cm/2in long) with striking five-petalled funnelled blooms of deep rich violet (2.5cm/1in long), with white, pink-tipped stamens. *R.* 'Fumiko' has purple flowers and *R.* 'Satschiko' has deep flame-orange flowers (both 80cm/32in); *R.* 'Rose Greeley' (90cm/3ft) has snowy white flowers.

> **BEST USES** Good for the mixed shrub or spring border and cottage gardens; elegant as colourful ground cover in shady corners and woodland gardens; ideal in pots, with ericaceous compost

FLOWERS April to May
SCENTED No
ASPECT Any, in a sheltered position; full sun to partial shade
SOIL Any fertile, humus-rich, well-drained acid soil
HARDINESS Fully hardy at temperatures down to -15°C/5°F; needs no winter protection
DROUGHT TOLERANCE Poor
PROBLEMS Aphids, caterpillars, leafhoppers, rhododendron whitefly and vine weevil; *Botrytis* (grey mould), bud blast, honey fungus, powdery mildew, petal blight, *Phytophthora* root rot and silver leaf
CARE Deadhead spent flowers to encourage healthy annual flower displays
PROPAGATION Semi-ripe cuttings in late summer

Vinca minor 'Atropurpurea' ♈
Lesser periwinkle

⬆ 15cm/6in ⬌ Indefinite   **EASY**

This neat, low-growing, evergreen shrublet from
Europe has trailing leaf stems with tough,
smooth, oval, shiny green leaves (5cm/2in long).
Vinca leaves can look unexciting, but this variety
has smooth, plum-coloured stems, topped with
simple, shallow, five-petalled, deep rich purple
flowers that handsomely stud the plant from
spring until early autumn and really enhance the
dark foliage, elevating it to classy ground cover.
It will grow in problem spots that other plants
won't cope with. *V.m.* f. *alba* 'Gertrude Jekyll' ♈
has white flowers; golden-leaved *V.m.*
'Illumination' has lilac blue flowers.

BEST USES Excellent ground cover for clothing
awkward shady banks or slopes; useful for
underplanting with spring bulbs; good for hanging
baskets and containers

FLOWERS April to September
SCENTED No
ASPECT Any, in a sheltered or exposed position; full sun
to full shade
SOIL Any fertile, moist, well-drained soil
HARDINESS Fully hardy at temperatures down to
-15°C/5°F; needs no winter protection
DROUGHT TOLERANCE Poor
PROBLEMS Rust
CARE Mulch with organic matter in spring; cut back hard
in spring to confine its spread (can be invasive)
PROPAGATION Division in spring or autumn; semi-ripe
cuttings in summer

Waldsteinia ternata

⬆ 10cm/4in ⬌ Indefinite   **EASY**

This spreading, mat-forming semi-evergreen
perennial can be found from Europe to Asia and
even Siberia. It has bright green tri-lobed leaves
(6cm/2½in long), resembling the foliage of a
strawberry plant, which are tinged bronze in mild
autumns and winters. In extreme winters, it may
lose some of its leaves. Loose clusters of cheerful,
shallow saucer-shaped buttercup yellow flowers
(1.5cm/½in) are held slightly above the leaves
and stud the foliage in spring. It is tough, happy
in sun or deep shade and able to adapt well to
different growing environments, making it
particularly useful as a dependable dense ground
cover plant in shade.

BEST USES Excellent ground cover for difficult
spots where almost nothing will grow; good in a
woodland garden or on shady slopes and banks

FLOWERS April to June
SCENTED No
ASPECT Any, in a sheltered position; full sun to
full shade
SOIL Any fertile, well-drained soil
HARDINESS Fully hardy at temperatures down to
-15°C/5°F; needs no winter protection
DROUGHT TOLERANCE Good, once established
PROBLEMS None
CARE Cut back at regular intervals to curb its spread
PROPAGATION Division in spring; sow seed in pots in
a cold frame in autumn

Aucuba japonica 'Crotonifolia' ♛
Spotted laurel

⬆ 3m/10ft ⬌ 3m/10ft   **EASY**

Laurels are the most widely planted hedging plant in the UK, or so I am told, and this evergreen shrub from Asia is elegant and compact, making a tidy, rounded shape. It has polished, leathery, slightly saw-edged, pointed oval mid-green leaves, splashed with creamy gold. The blooms are muted and restrained, comprising simple, star-shaped, deep maroon-red flowers, gathered in upright panicles, but it is grown for foliage rather than flowers. Laurels are easy to grow, largely unfussy about soil or aspect, and are low maintenance. *A.j.* 'Crassifolia' has deep green leaves; *A.j.* 'Golden King' ♛ has predominantly golden leaves.

BEST USES Ideal as hedging or windbreaks, in coastal and exposed gardens; good for mixed shrub borders, on city roof terraces and in pots

FLOWERS April; grown mainly for foliage
SCENTED No
ASPECT North, east or west facing, in a sheltered or exposed position; partial to full shade
SOIL Any fertile, moist, well-drained soil
HARDINESS Fully hardy at temperatures down to -15°C/5°F; needs no winter protection
DROUGHT TOLERANCE Excellent, once established
PROBLEMS None
CARE Remove dead, diseased or damaged wood in spring; trim hedges in spring; prune single shrubs back hard in spring
PROPAGATION Semi-ripe cuttings in late summer

Berberis × *stenophylla* ♛
Barberry

⬆ 4m/13ft ⬌ 4m/13ft   **EASY**

Barberries are found in hilly, rocky areas worldwide, and can be deciduous or evergreen. This dense, bushy, very prickly evergreen shrub has an upright habit, with arching brown stems, clothed in small, tough, leathery, elliptical, dark green leaves (2.5cm/1in long), with sharp thorns both along the stems and at the tips. In spring, it is generously attired with large, hanging, golden, lightly fragrant flower clusters, each bunch made up of small, dark yellow flowers (1cm/³⁄₈in across). Small rounded green berries (barberries) appear in summer, ageing to blue; although edible, they are unpleasantly acidic. The larger-leaved evergreen *B. julianae* ♛ is scented.

BEST USES Widely used as hedging (the prickles deter intruders) and especially good for coastal and exposed windy gardens; good in mixed spring borders; excellent for wildlife gardens

FLOWERS April to May
SCENTED Scented flowers
ASPECT Any, in a sheltered or exposed position; full sun to full shade
SOIL Any fertile, well-drained soil
HARDINESS Fully hardy at temperatures down to -15°C/5°F; needs no winter protection
DROUGHT TOLERANCE Excellent, once established
PROBLEMS Aphids; powdery mildew
CARE Trim both feature shrubs and hedges lightly after flowering
PROPAGATION Semi-ripe cuttings in summer

Choisya ternata Sundance ▼
Mexican orange blossom

⬆ 2.5m/8ft ⬌ 2.5m/8ft   **EASY**

Choisyas are handsome evergreen shrubs from Mexico. This densely attired, rounded variety has glossy oval leaves (8cm/3in long) and is the most golden of all the choisyas (the young leaves are noticeably bright yellow), though the colour dims in shade. Trademark sweetly fragrant, star-shaped, shallow, white flowers (3cm/1¼in across) are borne in generous clusters in late spring, with a second flush in summer and autumn, making it an all-round performer.

BEST USES Excellent in a hot, sunny mixed border; very effective ground cover on slopes and banks; makes an informal fragrant flowering hedge; pollution tolerant, so good for urban gardens; good for coastal gardens

FLOWERS May, with repeat flowering in August to September

SCENTED Scented flowers

ASPECT South, west or east facing, in a sheltered position; full sun to partial shade

SOIL Any fertile, well-drained soil

HARDINESS Fully hardy at temperatures down to -15°C/5°F; needs no winter protection

DROUGHT TOLERANCE Excellent, once established

PROBLEMS Slugs and snails may nibble young plants

CARE Trim lightly after flowering to maintain size and shape; takes hard pruning if it gets too big

PROPAGATION Semi-ripe cuttings in mid-summer to autumn

Embothrium coccineum Lanceolatum Group 'Ñorquinco' ▼
Chilean fire bush

⬆ 3m/10ft ⬌ 3m/10ft   **EASY**

This unusual, upright, multi-stemmed evergreen shrub or tree, with bold exotic flowers, has South American origins. The neat, lance-shaped, mid-green leaves (13cm/5in long) mature to deep green. Flamboyant, free-flowering, tubular scarlet flowers are produced in explosive fist-sized spidery clusters from late spring. It is borderline hardy (but becomes more frost tolerant with age) and slow in growth for the first three years.

BEST USES Excellent as hedging or screening (though you lose the flowers); good in an exotic garden or in woodland shade; ideal against a warm, sunny wall; good focal point on a lawn

FLOWERS May to June

SCENTED No

ASPECT South, west or east facing, in a sheltered position with protection from cold winds; full sun to partial shade

SOIL Any humus-rich, fertile, well-drained soil; add organic matter before planting

HARDINESS Fully hardy/borderline at temperatures down to -15°C/5°F; may need winter protection in cold areas

DROUGHT TOLERANCE Poor

PROBLEMS Cold winds can damage leaves

CARE Minimal; remove dead, diseased or damaged wood in late winter to early spring

PROPAGATION Greenwood cuttings in early summer; root cuttings in winter; detach and pot up rooted suckers in winter

Euphorbia characias subsp. *wulfenii* 🏅

⬆ 1.2m/4ft ⬌ 1.5m/5ft **EASY**

This architectural evergreen shrub from the Mediterranean provides striking form all year round. The upright stems are clothed with whorls of narrow grey-green leaves, with huge, domed, dazzling zingy lime green bracts rather than flower heads in spring; each small cupped flower has an appealing bronze-black eye. This is a low-maintenance plant for foliage lovers, making excellent vertical contrast to spreading plants.

BEST USES Ideal for architectural form and foliage in contemporary, Mediterranean and gravel gardens, as well as in traditional borders and cottage gardens; ideal for garden divisions

FLOWERS March to May
SCENTED No
ASPECT South, west or east facing, in a sheltered position; full sun
SOIL Any fertile, well-drained soil
HARDINESS Fully hardy at temperatures down to -15°C/5°F; needs no winter protection
DROUGHT TOLERANCE Excellent, once established
PROBLEMS None
CARE Cut the spent flower stems to ground level after flowering or in autumn; wear gloves to protect from irritating milky sap
PROPAGATION Division in early spring; basal stem cuttings in late spring or early summer

GREENFINGER TIP *Seal cuttings in warm water to stop the sap bleeding*

Leucothoe fontanesiana 🏅
Switch ivy

⬆ 2m/6ft ⬌ 3m/10ft **EASY**

This low-growing North American evergreen shrub is a shade lover, and infinitely useful for gloomy spaces. Its arching red branches are densely clothed with tough, leathery, oval deep green leaves (15cm/6in long), held on slim pink stems; new growth is often mottled with coppery-gold hues. White panicles of flowers (6cm/2½in long) are produced in reasonable numbers in spring. *L.f.* 'Rainbow', with marbled pink and white leaves and flowers, needs dappled sun to achieve its best colour; *L.f.* 'Rollissonii' 🏅 has white flowers and narrower leaves.

BEST USES Excellent ground cover on awkward banks and slopes; ideal for shady borders and woodland gardens; good for wildlife gardens, as pollinating insects love the flowers

FLOWERS April to May
SCENTED Scented flowers
ASPECT Any, in a sheltered or exposed position with protection from cold winds; partial shade
SOIL Any fertile, moist, humus-rich, well-drained acid soil
HARDINESS Fully hardy at temperatures down to -15°C/5°F; needs no winter protection
DROUGHT TOLERANCE Poor
PROBLEMS None
CARE Low maintenance; prune in winter, removing dead, diseased or damaged wood
PROPAGATION Semi-ripe cuttings in a heated propagator in summer

Lonicera nitida 'Baggesen's Gold' ♟
Poor man's box

⬆ 1.5m/5ft ⬌ 1.5m/5ft   **EASY**

This dense, evergreen shrub from China grows in thick, arching, lateral layers. It belongs to the honeysuckle family, and has small, oval, shiny golden leaves (1cm/⅜in long), which are different from the larger oval leaves of the climbing varieties. Tiny, twinned, lightly fragrant, tubular cream flowers, about the same size as the leaves, appear in spring. Light mauve, rounded berries are often produced in autumn. It is fast-growing. *L. nitida* has dark green leaves.

BEST USES Excellent for hedging and screening or as windbreaks in coastal, cottage or formal borders; good for wildlife gardens, where berries are foraged by birds

FLOWERS April
SCENTED Scented flowers
ASPECT Any, in a sheltered position; partial to full shade; foliage colour is best in sun
SOIL Any fertile, well-drained soil; add organic matter when planting to assist drought tolerance
HARDINESS Fully hardy at temperatures down to -15°C/5°F; needs no winter protection
DROUGHT TOLERANCE Good, once established
PROBLEMS Powdery mildew
CARE Trim after flowering to maintain size and shape; trim hedging three to four times a year
PROPAGATION Semi-ripe cuttings in late summer

Pieris 'Forest Flame' ♟

⬆ 4m/13ft ⬌ 2m/6ft   **EASY**

If you have acid soil, this is a great foliage plant. It's a neat, compact, rounded evergreen shrub from Asia with chameleon colouring: the glossy young leaflets are flamed vivid red in early spring, turning to pink and cream, before maturing to deep green lance-shaped leaves (13cm/5in long). Tiny bell-shaped white flowers droop in heavy bead-like clusters (15cm/6in long) as the flowers open in spring. *P.* 'Flaming Silver' ♟ (65cm/25in) is compact, with creamy green variegated foliage.

BEST USES Excellent for the cottage garden or woodland; ideal for covering banks that are awkward to mow; good in pots and containers in dappled city gardens

FLOWERS April to May; grown mainly for foliage
SCENTED No
ASPECT South, west or east facing, in a sheltered position with protection from cold winds; full sun to partial shade
SOIL Any fertile, moist, well-drained acid soil
HARDINESS Frost hardy at temperatures down to -5°C/23°F; may need winter protection
DROUGHT TOLERANCE Excellent, once established
PROBLEMS Leaf spot and Phytophthora root rot
CARE Trim lightly after flowering to maintain size and shape
PROPAGATION Semi-ripe cuttings in a heated propagator in late summer

Piptanthus nepalensis
Evergreen laburnum

⬆ 2.5m/8ft ↔ 2m/6ft   MEDIUM

This multi-stemmed, rounded, upright evergreen shrub from the Himalayas is truly delightful, but can be short-lived, no doubt due to its energetic growing habit. It has handsome, tri-lobed, shiny deep green leaves (15cm/6in long), with blue-green undersides, on woody brown stems. In spring, furry-stemmed flower buds blossom to reveal sunshiny yellow pea-like flowers (4cm/1½in long) in cheery clusters, very much like laburnum blossom, followed by decorative dangling, flat, greeny yellow pea pods. It is frost hardy, so will do better in mild areas, but if you can offer it a sheltered wall, give it a go.

BEST USES Ideal trained as a wall shrub; good for spring borders mixed with blue and white planting schemes; perfect for cottage and woodland gardens

FLOWERS May to June
SCENTED No
ASPECT Any, in a sheltered position with protection from winds; full sun to partial shade
SOIL Any fertile, well-drained soil
HARDINESS Frost hardy at temperatures down to -5°C/23°F; may need winter protection
DROUGHT TOLERANCE Poor
PROBLEMS None; older leaves yellow and look tatty by spring
CARE Low maintenance; remove dead, diseased or damaged wood in late winter or early spring when necessary
PROPAGATION Heeled semi-ripe cuttings in summer

Rhaphiolepis umbellata ♟
Japanese hawthorn

⬆ 1.5m/5ft ↔ 1.5m/5ft   EASY

The restrained formality of this neat, rounded, elegant evergreen shrub is a clue to its Asian origins. Its oval leaves (10cm/4in long) are glossy and deep green, and the small, simple, gappy, flat white flowers, often flushed pale pink, are held in fragrant, honey-scented panicles (10cm/4in long) in spring. It finishes its growing season with rounded black berries, which follow after the flowers. A wizard year-rounder.

BEST USES Excellent for formal borders, cottage and city gardens; ideal as a small, neat hedge; good for pots and containers

FLOWERS April to May
SCENTED Scented flowers
ASPECT South or west facing, in a sheltered position with protection from cold winds; full sun
SOIL Any fertile, moist, well-drained soil
HARDINESS Frost hardy at temperatures down to -5°C/23°F; may need winter protection
DROUGHT TOLERANCE Excellent, once established
PROBLEMS None
CARE Prune lightly after flowering to maintain size and shape
PROPAGATION Semi-ripe cuttings in late summer; layering in autumn

GREENFINGER TIP *Although this plant prefers full sun, try it in light shade: there will be fewer flowers, but the foliage will remain handsome*

Rhododendron yakushimanum 'Koichiro Wada' ⚊

⬆ 1.2m/4ft ⬌ 1.2m/4ft   EASY

This compact, domed, evergreen shrub from Japan is densely clothed in lance-shaped deep green leaves with bristly, cinnamon-coloured undersides. Pale pink buds jewel the bush in spring, opening to clusters of bell-shaped pale pinky white flowers (each flower about 5cm/2in long). In ideal conditions this will reach its full size within five years. *R.* 'Kalinka' (candy pink flowers), *R.* 'Golden Wedding' (apricot flowers) and *R.* 'Silver Sixpence' (creamy white flowers) are a similar size.

> **BEST USES** Excellent for formal borders, as well as cottage, city, Oriental and woodland gardens; ideal as a hedge or screening; good in pots

FLOWERS May to June
SCENTED No
ASPECT Any, in a sheltered position with protection from cold winds; partial shade
SOIL Any fertile, humus-rich, moist, well-drained acid soil
HARDINESS Fully hardy at temperatures down to -15°C/5°F; needs no winter protection
DROUGHT TOLERANCE Poor
PROBLEMS Aphids, caterpillars, leafhoppers, rhododendron whitefly and vine weevil; *Botrytis* (grey mould), bud blast, honey fungus, powdery mildew, petal blight, *Phytophthora* root rot and silver leaf
CARE Prune lightly after flowering to maintain size and shape
PROPAGATION Semi-ripe cuttings in late summer; layering in autumn

Rosmarinus officinalis 'Miss Jessopp's Upright' ⚊   **Rosemary**

⬆ 2m/6ft ⬌ 2m/6ft   EASY

This familiar and widely grown bushy, upright, aromatic evergreen shrub from the Mediterranean has trademark small, narrow, needle-like, dark green leaves with silver grey undersides (5cm/2in long), which colour best when planted in full sun. Small, pale powder-blue flowers (1cm/⅜in long), with curved lilac stamens, charmingly cluster the stems from spring to summer. *R.o.* 'Primley Blue' (90cm/3ft) is more compact and *R.o.* Prostratus Group (50cm/20in) is a low-growing, spreading variety; both have the typical pale blue flowers.

> **BEST USES** Ideal for sunny borders, dry banks, coastal and Mediterranean gardens; excellent in pots outside the kitchen door; ideal for the wildlife garden, attracting bees and butterflies; useful as low hedging and for informal garden divisions

FLOWERS April to June
SCENTED Aromatic leaves
ASPECT South or west facing, in a sheltered position; full sun
SOIL Any fertile, well-drained soil
HARDINESS Frost hardy at temperatures down to -5°C/23°F; may need winter protection
DROUGHT TOLERANCE Excellent, once established
PROBLEMS Aphids and froghoppers; honey fungus
CARE Trim lightly after flowering, to retain its bushy habit and prevent it becoming leggy
PROPAGATION Sow seed in pots in a cold frame in spring; semi-ripe cuttings in summer

Skimmia x *confusa* 'Kew Green' ♗

⬆ 1.5m/5ft ⬌ 1.5m/5ft   **EASY**

This domed evergreen shrub of Asian origin is thickly clothed with lance-shaped deep green leaves (10cm/4in long), and looks neat and tidy all year round. In spring, fragrant, flowering spires (15cm/6in long) are formed from tiny, tubular, creamy flowers, giving the impression the whole shrub (which is male, incidentally) is covered in blossom. *S. japonica* 'Kew White' (1.5m/5ft) has fragrant white flowers and white berries; *S.j.* 'Rubella' ♗ (1.5m/5ft) has scented red-flushed white flowers.

BEST USES Unbeatable camouflage for awkward slopes and banks; great in shady woodland or city gardens; ideal for north-facing patios and courtyards

FLOWERS April to May

SCENTED Scented flowers

ASPECT Any, in a sheltered or exposed position; full sun to full shade

SOIL Any fertile, well-drained soil

HARDINESS Fully hardy at temperatures down to -15°C/5°F; needs no winter protection

DROUGHT TOLERANCE Poor

PROBLEMS Scale insect

CARE Trim lightly after flowering to maintain size and shape

PROPAGATION Semi-ripe cuttings in a heated propagator in late summer

GREENFINGER TIP *In small spaces, you can keep this trimmed to a height of 50cm/20in*

Ulex europaeus
Common gorse

⬆ 2.5m/8ft ⬌ 2m/6ft   **EASY**

This very dense, mounded, evergreen shrub from western Europe, with narrow, spiny, deep green leaves (2.5cm/1in long), is a familiar sight growing wild on sandy heaths and roadsides. Its crowning glory are the coconut-scented, gaudy yellow pea-like flowers (2cm/¾in long), borne in such profusion in spring that you can barely see the foliage. It is at its best during the frenzied flowering of spring, but it flowers intermittently throughout the year. Many nesting birds raise their young in gorse bushes as they offer an impregnable fortress from predators.

BEST USES Ideal in coastal gardens as hedging or windbreaks; perfect for the wildlife garden, and madly attractive to bees

FLOWERS April to June

SCENTED Scented flowers

ASPECT Any, in a sheltered or exposed position; full sun

SOIL Any fertile, well-drained soil

HARDINESS Fully hardy at temperatures down to -15°C/5°F; needs no winter protection

DROUGHT TOLERANCE Excellent, once established

PROBLEMS None

CARE Cut out faded flower spikes and old dead growth in spring

PROPAGATION Pre-soak seed and sow in pots in a cold frame in spring or autumn; greenwood cuttings in early to mid-summer; hardwood cuttings in late autumn to mid-winter

Clematis armandii 'Snowdrift'
Virgin's bower

⬆ 5m/16ft ⬌ 3m/10ft   **EASY**

This tendrilled evergreen climber from Asia is a fast grower, with trademark long, strappy leaves that are an appealing glossy deep green. The plethora of almond-scented star-shaped pure white flowers (5cm/2in across), with pale lemon centres, makes this a plant to covet when skies are grey. It is an invaluable addition to the spring garden and will prove handy for masking unattractive garden features.

BEST USES Excellent for screening walls, fences and unsightly areas; ideal for sunny walls, pergolas and arbours; good for wildflower and cottage gardens as well as sheltered city patios and country courtyards; good in containers

FLOWERS March to April

SCENTED Scented flowers

ASPECT South or west facing, in a sheltered position with protection from winds; full sun to partial shade

SOIL Any fertile, well-drained soil

HARDINESS Frost hardy at temperatures down to -5°C/23°F; may need winter protection

DROUGHT TOLERANCE Poor

PROBLEMS Earwigs and caterpillars may nibble young growth; clematis wilt

CARE Needs no pruning; if absolutely necessary, prune unwanted stems and stragglers immediately after flowering (Group1)

PROPAGATION Division in autumn

Griselinia littoralis ⚥

⬆ 8m/26ft ⬌ 5m/16ft   **EASY**

This upright evergreen shrub from New Zealand has handsome, tough, rounded, polished bright apple green leaves (10cm/4in long). Negligible small green flowers are borne in clusters in spring, with male and female flowers on separate bushes. When plants of both sexes are grown, clusters of rounded purple-black berries are produced in autumn. This shrub is gaining popularity as hedging and has a reasonable growth rate (some 30cm/12in each year), but may need protection in winter in cold areas. *G.l.* 'Variegata' ⚥ (3m/10ft) has emerald green and silvery white marbled leaves; *G.l.* 'Dixon's Cream' (3m/10ft) has green leaves with creamy splashes.

BEST USES Excellent as hedging or screening in formal gardens or coastal areas; good foliage for exotic planting schemes

FLOWERS May

SCENTED No

ASPECT South or west facing, in a sheltered or exposed position; full sun

SOIL Any fertile, well-drained soil

HARDINESS Fully hardy/borderline at temperatures down to -15°C/5°F; may need winter protection in cold areas

DROUGHT TOLERANCE Excellent, once established

PROBLEMS Leaf spot

CARE Lightly trim plants to maintain size and spread in mid to late spring

PROPAGATION Semi-ripe cuttings in summer

Laurus nobilis 🏅
Bay laurel/Sweet bay

⬆ 12m/40ft ⬌ 10m/32ft　　　　**EASY**

Most of us will instantly recognise this conical evergreen tree or large shrub from the Mediterranean, with its highly polished, oval, aromatic deep green leaves (10cm/4in long). In spring, numerous clusters of tiny, shallow, cupped, pale yellow flowers (6mm/¼in across), with deeper yellow stamens, peep bashfully through the foliage, followed by small, rounded, black berries on female plants. *L.n.* 'Aurea' 🏅 has golden foliage.

> **BEST USES** Excellent for hedging or as a specimen plant in a formal lawn; good as a wall shrub; ideal in a container for topiary; ideal for mild coastal gardens; attractive to bees

FLOWERS April to May

SCENTED Aromatic leaves

ASPECT South, west or east facing, in a sheltered position with protection from winds; full sun to partial shade

SOIL Any fertile, moist, well-drained soil

HARDINESS Frost hardy at temperatures down to -5°/23°F; may need winter protection

DROUGHT TOLERANCE Excellent, once established

PROBLEMS Bay suckers, scale insect and tortrix moth caterpillars; powdery mildew

CARE Prune out dead, diseased or damaged material in late winter or early spring; clip topiary in early to mid summer

PROPAGATION Semi-ripe cuttings in summer

Osmanthus delavayi 🏅
Delavay tea olive

⬆ 6m/20ft ⬌ 4m/13ft　　　　**EASY**

This neat, rounded, slow-growing evergreen shrub of Chinese origin has arching stems, densely clothed with tough, polished dark green leaves (2.5cm/1in long), with serrated edges. Come spring, it is generously hung with clusters of small, tubular, highly fragrant, pure white flowers (1cm/³⁄₈in across) that scent the air enticingly. Although not produced in great number, rounded purple-black berries follow the flowers. It is an elegant shrub for all seasons. There are also many other choice species, including *O.* × *burkwoodii* 🏅 (3m/10ft) and the holly-leaved *O. heterophyllus* (5m/16ft).

> **BEST USES** Excellent as evergreen structure for year-round interest in a formal border, woodland garden or shrubbery; ideal for hedging and screening or as topiary

FLOWERS April to May

SCENTED Scented flowers

ASPECT Any, in a sheltered or exposed position; full sun to partial shade

SOIL Any fertile, well-drained soil

HARDINESS Fully hardy at temperatures down to -15°/5°F; needs no winter protection

DROUGHT TOLERANCE Good, once established

PROBLEMS None

CARE Minimal pruning; cut out dead, diseased or damaged material in spring; cut hedges in spring

PROPAGATION Semi-ripe cuttings in a heated propagator in summer

Phillyrea latifolia
Mock privet/Green olive

⬆ 9m/30ft ⬌ 9m/30ft — EASY

This is a very handsome, architectural evergreen shrub from Japan that has a dense, rounded habit, with leathery, oval, glossy, grey-green leaves (6cm/2½in long). In late spring, unremarkable small clusters of greenish flowers pack a punch in the fragrance department, emanating a delightful fruity perfume. Small, rounded, green miniature olive-like berries follow the flowers, maturing to purple-black. It has a medium rate of growth and is very useful in landscaping, as it is such an elegant plant.

BEST USES Excellent for hedging, and often used for topiary, as an architectural focal point; ideal for coastal, Mediterranean, gravel and woodland gardens

FLOWERS May to June

SCENTED Scented flowers

ASPECT Any, in a sheltered or exposed position; full sun to partial shade

SOIL Any fertile, moist, well-drained soil

HARDINESS Fully hardy at temperatures down to -15°C/5°F; needs no winter protection

DROUGHT TOLERANCE Excellent, once established

PROBLEMS Aphids (whitefly)

CARE Prune in late winter or early spring, or trim lightly after flowering

PROPAGATION Semi-ripe cuttings in a heated propagator in summer

GREENFINGER TIP *In a cold region, try this instead of the Mediterranean olive (Olea europaea)*

Photinia x *fraseri* 'Red Robin' 🎖

⬆ 5m/16ft ⬌ 5m/16ft — EASY

This upright, formal, evergreen Asian shrub has polished, oval, soft red young leaves, which mature to deeper green later in the year and are up to 20cm/8in long. It is spring-flowering, bearing branching panicles of small white flowers on attractive purple stems, though they are not so alluring that you would plant it for the blooms. Small round berries follow the flowers. It is fairly fast growing (30cm/12in per year) and is increasingly popular as a hedging plant.

BEST USES Good for hedging or screening; excellent in large containers on gloomy patios or roof gardens; makes lively ground cover in shady corners or on awkward slopes and banks

FLOWERS April to May; grown mainly for foliage

SCENTED No

ASPECT Any, in a sheltered or exposed position; full sun to partial shade

SOIL Any fertile, moist, well-drained soil

HARDINESS Fully hardy at temperatures down to -15°C/5°F; needs no winter protection

DROUGHT TOLERANCE Excellent, once established

PROBLEMS Fireblight, leaf spot and powdery mildew; may not flower in shade

CARE Low maintenance; trim hedges or remove any unwanted, dead, diseased or damaged growth in late winter to early spring; nip out the young shoot tips to encourage deep red leaflets

PROPAGATION Semi-ripe cuttings in a heated propagator in summer

Pittosporum tobira
Japanese mock orange

⬆ 10m/32ft ↔ 3m/10ft   EASY

This dense, bushy, rounded evergreen shrub of New Zealand origin is stylish and restrained, making it perfect for adding formality to the garden. It has polished, leathery, wavy-edged deep green leaves (10cm/4in long) and small, simple, starry-shaped ivory flowers (2.5cm/1in across) that make large clusters in spring. These deliver sweet fragrance before ageing to buttery yellow, and are followed by rounded tan berries. When grown in a large container this will reach a height of about 2m/6ft rather than the full mature size, so it should prove infinitely manageable in smaller gardens.

BEST USES Excellent in a woodland, cottage or formal garden; ideal as hedging; good in containers in city gardens

FLOWERS May to June
SCENTED Scented flowers
ASPECT Any, in a sheltered position with protection from cold winds; full sun to partial shade
SOIL Any fertile, moist, well-drained soil
HARDINESS Frost hardy at temperatures down to 5°/23°F; may need winter protection
DROUGHT TOLERANCE Good, once established
PROBLEMS Scale insect; leaf spot and powdery mildew
CARE Low maintenance; remove dead, diseased or damaged material in late winter or early spring; trim hedges in spring or summer
PROPAGATION Semi-ripe cuttings in summer

Rhamnus alaternus
Italian buckthorn

⬆ 5m/15ft ↔ 4m/13ft   EASY

This fast-growing, upright evergreen shrub from the Mediterranean has very attractive oval glossy dark green leaves (7cm/2¾in long). The tiny, almost bauble-like, yellow-green flowers produced in spring to summer are fairly insignificant, and are followed by small, rounded red berries that ripen to black. These add year-round interest for wildlife gardeners and birds alike. This is a classy, versatile shrub that is easy to grow. *R. alaternus* 'Argenteovariegata' (4m/13ft) is slightly smaller, with variegated leaves.

BEST USES Ideal as hedging or screening in coastal and cottage gardens; works well as a free-standing or wall shrub in large borders

FLOWERS May to June
SCENTED No
ASPECT South or west facing, in a sheltered position; full sun to partial shade
SOIL Any fertile, well-drained soil
HARDINESS Frost hardy at temperatures down to -5°C/23°F; may need winter protection
DROUGHT TOLERANCE Excellent, once established
PROBLEMS None
CARE Remove dead, diseased or damaged wood in late winter to early spring
PROPAGATION Semi-ripe cuttings in summer

Ferns

Ferns are over 360 million years old. When skies were patrolled by armour-plated pterodactyls, oceans roiled with vicious fish lizards and dinosaurs roamed the earth, ancient ferns stood trembling underfoot.

They are tough, architectural, foliage plants with fantastic textures and the most beautifully diverse leaves (or fronds). Some are deciduous and die back every year, but there are plenty of evergreen species to tempt the creative gardener, with something for nearly every area of the garden; they grow in crevices, in paving cracks, shady woodlands and wetlands.

They tend to prefer acid soils, but there are still a great many that can cope with limey or clay soils. Most appreciate a moist, humus-rich soil and, crucially, moist air but, perhaps surprisingly, some are tolerant of dry shade and drought. For example, *Asplenium scolopendrium* will grow in cracks at the base of old walls, presumably getting moisture from the mortar. They are pest free and thrive with very little maintenance (just trim away damaged leaves in late winter or early spring, as the new fronds emerge). Ferns are unlike any other plants on our planet. They don't produce pollen or seeds and instead spread by rhizomes or via spore dispersal.

As well as the ferns described in detail here, try *Dryopteris affinis* 'Cristata' ♀ in damp places – it has elegant, shuttlecock formation pale green fronds unfurling in spring, maturing to dark green with age, and chestnut ribbing (90cm/3ft); the easy-going British native, *Polypodium vulgare* (30cm/12in), is as tough as old boots, will grow anywhere sheltered and has mid-green triangular fronds; and *Polystichum setiferum* Divisilobum Group 'Dahlem' is great for dry shade, with lettuce green leaves in rosette formation (75cm/30in).

Asplenium scolopendrium ♀
Hart's tongue fern

⬆ 70cm/28in ⬌ 60cm/24in · · · · · · · · · · EASY

This rhizomatous evergreen perennial, originally from Europe to North America and Asia, is one of the few ferns whose leaves are not dissected or divided; it has smooth, glossy green leaves all year round. Architectural juvenile fronds unfurl in early spring, revealing long, ribbon-like, slightly wavy-edged, polished, deeply veined deep green leaves (which can reach 40cm/16in in length). The bases of the leaves are arrow-shaped and maroon-brown spores stripe the undersides. *A.s.* Cristatum Group (90cm/3ft) has broader, lettuce-like frilly leaves; *A.s.* 'Kaye's Lacerated' ♀ (60cm/24in) has wider, leathery, ultra-frilly bright green leaves.

> **BEST USES** Ideal for gloomy corners and as focal plants in a shady woodland garden; great for clothing awkward slopes; perfect for formal borders and cottage gardens; good in containers

FLOWERS Non-flowering; grown for foliage
SCENTED No
ASPECT Any, in a sheltered or exposed position; partial to full shade
SOIL Any fertile, humus-rich, well-drained soil
HARDINESS Fully hardy at temperatures down to -15°C/5°F; needs no winter protection
DROUGHT TOLERANCE Good, once established
PROBLEMS Slugs and snails
CARE In winter or early spring, remove tatty leaves
PROPAGATION Division in early spring

Blechnum spicant

Hard fern

⬆ 50cm/20in ⬌ 60cm/24in   **EASY**

This evergreen fern from Europe and Asia is found growing wild in woods, rocky areas and banks, and spreads by creeping rhizomes. It has handsome, shiny, upright, deeply divided dark green fronds (50cm/20in long) that are slightly leathery to the touch. As the fern matures, the older fronds lean out in a graceful arching manner, leaving the younger summer growth upright in the centre like an exploding green fountain. It is relatively unfussy about soil, putting up with everything from dry sandy soil to heavy clay.

BEST USES Great on banks and awkward slopes; good as woodland ground cover; excellent in any flower border, including contemporary, formal or cottage gardens

FLOWERS Non-flowering; grown for foliage
SCENTED No
ASPECT Any, in a sheltered or exposed position; full sun to full shade
SOIL Any fertile, well-drained soil
HARDINESS Fully hardy at temperatures down to -15°C/5°F; needs no winter protection
DROUGHT TOLERANCE Good, once established
PROBLEMS None
CARE In summer to autumn, remove the outer leaves when they start to look tatty, cutting the untidy fronds at the base of their stems
PROPAGATION Division in spring

Polypodium cambricum 'Richard Kayse'

Wintergreen fern

⬆ 45cm/18in ⬌ 30cm/12in   **EASY**

This fern is a native evergreen perennial with tough, flattened, very deeply divided mid-green fronds (60cm/24in long), like delightfully lacy filigreed shuttlecocks. You may have to hunt around to find it, but more than a handful of nurseries now stock it. *P.c.* Pulcherrimum Group 'Pulcherrimnum Addison' (30cm/12in) has very pretty pale green lacy fronds.

BEST USES Ideal as ground cover in woodland gardens or in dappled shade in small city courtyards and cottage gardens; good in pots

FLOWERS Non-flowering; grown for foliage
SCENTED No
ASPECT Any, in a sheltered position with protection from strong winds; full sun to partial shade
SOIL Any fertile, well-drained, stony or humus-rich soil
HARDINESS Fully hardy at temperatures down to -15°C/5°F; needs no winter protection
DROUGHT TOLERANCE Poor
PROBLEMS None
CARE In winter or early spring, remove tatty leaves
PROPAGATION Division in early autumn

GREENFINGER TIP *When dividing, cut the clump into a few good-sized pieces with roots and foliage attached to each section, as small sections will struggle to survive*

FERNS

Polystichum munitum ♟
Sword fern

⬆ 90cm/3ft ⬌ 1.2m/4ft EASY

This tough, architectural, clump-forming evergreen perennial comes from North America. It is tall and needs plenty of space – don't crowd it, so you can really appreciate its sculptural qualities. It has a lovely upright stance and a clean, contemporary shape, with fresh, rich green, leathery, tapering, deeply cut divided fronds (90cm/3ft long), graphically embossed with fresh green spores on the undersides, which darken to felty tan. It will take any soil as long as it is in a cool, shady spot.

BEST USES Wonderful as a background foil for woodland plantings; good by shady ponds and streams

FLOWERS Non-flowering; grown for foliage
SCENTED No
ASPECT Any, in a sheltered or exposed position; partial to full shade
SOIL Any fertile, moist, humus-rich, well-drained soil
HARDINESS Fully hardy at temperatures down to -15°C/5°F; needs no winter protection
DROUGHT TOLERANCE Poor
PROBLEMS None
CARE In winter or early spring, remove any tatty fronds as necessary
PROPAGATION Division in spring

Polystichum setiferum ♟
Soft shield fern

⬆ 1.2m/4ft ⬌ 90cm/3ft EASY

This architectural, rhizomatous evergreen perennial from Europe has large, sculptural, deeply cut, tapering, deep green fronds that unfurl to reveal their full elegant height. It is reliably tolerant of dry shade. *P.s.* 'Pulcherrimum Bevis' ♟ (80cm/32in) is more compact; *P.s.* Plumosodivisilobum Group has finely cut soft fresh green fronds with appealing ginger-coloured stems.

BEST USES Good as graceful, textural background in the woodland or wildlife garden, herbaceous border or contemporary garden; masks the unattractive dieback of flowering bulbs

FLOWERS Non-flowering; grown for foliage
SCENTED No
ASPECT Any, in a sheltered or exposed position; partial to full shade
SOIL Any fertile, humus-rich, moist, well-drained soil; add organic matter before planting
HARDINESS Fully hardy at temperatures down to -15°C/5°F; needs no winter protection
DROUGHT TOLERANCE Good, once established
PROBLEMS None
CARE In winter or early spring, remove all the brittle, dead fronds from the previous year
PROPAGATION Division in spring

SUMMER

The wonderful thing about evergreen plants is that you know you can rely on their foliage year round – but summer is the time when the sage grey and silver-leaved evergreens really come into their own. Their pungent, Mediterranean aromas hang headily in the air, while their heightened silvered foliage seems to shimmer in the afternoon heat.

This is also the time when the ornamental grasses are at their best, languidly stirred by warm, gentle breezes, adding height and texture to the summer border.

Acaena microphylla 'Kupferteppich'
New Zealand burr

⬆ 90cm/3ft ⬌ 90cm/3ft · · · · · · · · · · · · **EASY**

An attractive, mat-forming, evergreen alpine perennial, this is found hugging nooks and crannies on mountains and hillsides across the southern hemisphere. It has small, toothed, grey-green leaves with bronze overtones (3cm/1¼in long) which make a pleasing compact russet carpet by the end of summer; purplish tints appear with the onset of winter. Curious reddish-brown burrs (2cm/¾in across), resembling small sea urchins, appear in late summer, on short, straight slender pinky brown stems held above the carpet of foliage. It is less invasive than others of its kind.

BEST USES Useful ground cover on banks or in rockeries; good in gaps in dry stone walls or between paving stones; ideal for troughs or pots

FLOWERS August

SCENTED No

ASPECT Any, in a sheltered position; full sun to partial shade

SOIL Any fertile, moist, well-drained soil

HARDINESS Fully hardy at temperatures down to -15°C/5°F; needs no winter protection

DROUGHT TOLERANCE Excellent, once established

PROBLEMS None

CARE Trim lightly after flowering to maintain spread and shape

PROPAGATION Detach and pot up rooted plantlets in early spring or autumn; sow seed in pots in a cold frame in autumn

Anemanthele lessoniana (formerly *Stipa arundinacea*) Pheasant's tail grass

⬆ 90cm/3ft ⬌ 1.2m/4ft **EASY**

This architectural, rhizomatous evergreen grass from New Zealand has narrow, grass-like dark green leaves (30cm/12in long), which take on an appealing rusty-copper flush in summer and into winter. Its fountaining, airy, gossamer-fine flower panicles top deeply arching stems (75cm/30in long) from summer into autumn; they sway in the slightest breeze, causing the tips of the flowers to gently sweep the ground. Most stipas prefer full sun, but this is happy with light shade as long as the soil is well drained. An exceptional plant, with fabulous foliage: 10/10.

BEST USES Excellent for adding texture to prairie planting and gravel gardens, borders or wildflower gardens; survives well in containers

FLOWERS June to September

SCENTED No

ASPECT Any, in a sheltered or exposed position; full sun to partial shade

SOIL Any fertile, well-drained soil

HARDINESS Fully hardy at temperatures down to -15°C/5°F; needs no winter protection

DROUGHT TOLERANCE Excellent, once established

PROBLEMS None

CARE Cut back the flowering stalks in late winter; comb through with your fingers in early spring to remove dead or tatty growth

PROPAGATION Self-seeds freely; division in early spring; sow seed in pots in a cold frame in spring

Campanula portenschlagiana Dalmation bellflower

⬆ 15cm/6in ⬌ 60cm/24in **EASY**

Campanulas offer something for everyone, from small ground-hugging species to tall, handsome border plants, but many are not evergreen. This fast-growing, cascading, evergreen alpine perennial from Croatia has a toughness that belies the daintiness of its heart-shaped mid-green leaves (4cm/1½in long) and the delicate nodding habit of the rich purple belled flowers (2cm/¾in long). The summer flowering is so profuse that the flowers often eclipse the foliage; it remains tidy, dense and green in winter. I've seen it growing in the mortar at the top of house walls, so it thrives on neglect.

BEST USES Great for rocky banks, or crevices in stone and brick walls and between paving slabs; useful as edging; happy in pots and containers

FLOWERS July to August

SCENTED No

ASPECT Any, in a sheltered or exposed position; full sun to partial shade

SOIL Any fertile, well-drained soil

HARDINESS Fully hardy at temperatures down to -15°C/5°F; needs no winter protection

DROUGHT TOLERANCE Excellent, once established

PROBLEMS Slugs and snails; powdery mildew and rust

CARE Deadhead after flowering, to maintain dense foliage growth

PROPAGATION Division in spring or autumn; sow seed in pots in a cold frame in autumn

Cistus x *purpureus* 'Alan Fradd'
Rock rose

⬆ 90cm/3ft ⬌ 90cm/3ft   **EASY**

Rock roses are good-natured, evergreen shrubs from dry, stony lands between southern Europe, Greece and Turkey. This hybrid has a rounded habit, with tough, coarse, oval, aromatic, sage green leaves (10cm/4in long), with crimped edges. The tissue-papery white flowers (4.5cm/1¾in across), with maroon blotches at the centre and golden stamens, are held on reddish-brown stems and last only a day, but they are numerous, generously studding the shrub like exotic jewels. Each new day brings another crop of flowers. Bliss.

BEST USES Unbeatable ground cover for rocky banks, piles of rubble and hot, dry spots; excellent in hot, sunny borders and in Mediterranean or gravel gardens; good in pots

FLOWERS June to July
SCENTED Aromatic leaves
ASPECT Any, in a sheltered position; full sun
SOIL Any fertile to poor, well-drained soil
HARDINESS Frost hardy at temperatures down to -5°C/23°F; may need winter protection
DROUGHT TOLERANCE Excellent, once established
PROBLEMS None
CARE Deadhead after flowering; trim back lightly after flowering to keep growth bushy
PROPAGATION Softwood cuttings in summer; sow ripe seed immediately in pots in a cold frame

Convolvulus cneorum 🏆
Silverbush

⬆ 60cm/24in ⬌ 75cm/30in   **EASY**

This evergreen shrub from the Mediterranean makes a tidy, rounded mound of oval, silky, silver grey leaves (6cm/2½in long). Among its endearing features are pinkish, tightly furled umbrella-like coned flower buds that open up in early summer to reveal an abundance of large, white, trumpet-shaped flowers (4cm/1½in across) with yellow centres. It is far superior to its notorious bindweed relatives, and lacks their invasive tendencies.

BEST USES Great in rock gardens, alpine beds and Mediterranean or gravel gardens; good in a traditional herbaceous border, where its colour is an effective foil for blue, purple and yellow flowers

FLOWERS May to July
SCENTED No
ASPECT South or west facing, in a sheltered position; full sun
SOIL Any gritty, fertile, well-drained soil
HARDINESS Frost hardy at temperatures down to -5°C/23°F; may need winter protection
DROUGHT TOLERANCE Excellent, once established
PROBLEMS None
CARE Best left to its own devices; trim lightly in autumn, after flowering, to retain its bushy appearance and prevent it becoming straggly
PROPAGATION Semi-ripe cuttings in summer or early autumn

Daboecia cantabrica subsp. *scotica* 'Silverwells' ♈ Silverwells heath

↑ 15cm/6in ↔ 35cm/14in　　　　　EASY

This small European evergreen shrub can be commonly found growing wild on exposed heathlands, cliffs and mountains in Ireland. It has tiny oval deep green leaves (8mm/³/₈in long) and is smothered in generous numbers of small white flowers, like upturned bells (it would be more aptly named 'silver bells'), about the same size as the leaves, from late spring. *D.c.* subsp. *s.* 'William Buchanan' ♈ has deep crimson flowers.

BEST USES Desirable ground cover for acid soils; useful on banks and slopes; good in pots

FLOWERS May to September (often to first frosts)
SCENTED No
ASPECT Any, in a sheltered or exposed position; full sun to partial shade
SOIL Any fertile, moist, well-drained acid soil
HARDINESS Fully hardy at temperatures down to -15°C/5°F; needs no winter protection
DROUGHT TOLERANCE Good, once established
PROBLEMS *Phytophthora* root rot
CARE Trim lightly in early spring or after flowering
PROPAGATION Semi-ripe cuttings in mid-summer

GREENFINGER TIP *I've grown these in pots of loamy compost in light shade: they flowered less profusely but will make do in a light, neutral soil*

Festuca glauca 'Elijah Blue'
Blue fescue

↑ 10cm/4in ↔ 10cm/4in　　　　　EASY

This compact but very architectural evergreen grass from south-west Europe has narrow, thin, grassy, silver, almost metallic blue, blades (20cm/8in long) that make small, low, textural hummocks. It produces small, bluish panicles in summer that turn to beige with age. The leaf colour is always heightened when planted in a hot, sunny spot. *F.g.* 'Blaufuchs' ♈ (syn. Blue Fox) (30cm/12in tall) has steely blue leaves; *F.g.* 'Golden Toupee' (45cm/18in) has bright green-gold foliage.

BEST USES Excellent ground cover, densely planted in a gravel or Mediterranean garden; ideal as edging; good in pots and containers in modern city gardens

FLOWERS June to July
SCENTED No
ASPECT Any, in a sheltered or exposed position; full sun
SOIL Any moderately fertile to poor, well-drained soil
HARDINESS Fully hardy at temperatures down to -15°C/5°F; needs no winter protection
DROUGHT TOLERANCE Excellent, once established
PROBLEMS None
CARE Rake through the grass with your fingers in winter to remove the dead leaves; divide every three years or so, as it can become tatty with age
PROPAGATION Division in spring; sow seed in pots in a cold frame from spring to autumn

Geranium endressii
Hardy geranium

⬆ 45cm/18in ⬌ 60cm/24in   **EASY**

This clump-forming, rhizomatous evergreen perennial from the Pyrenees forms pleasing clumps of rose-scented, deeply lobed, heavily veined mid-green leaves (15cm/6in long). Slim stems hold shallow trumpet-shaped, clear pale pink flowers (4cm/1½in across) that mature to deeper pink as they age. Like all hardy geraniums, it is tolerant of almost all soils, except the very waterlogged, and is shade tolerant. *G.e.* 'Castle Drogo' ♟ has peach-coloured flowers; *G.e.* 'Rose' has pale green foliage with pale rose-coloured flowers.

BEST USES Excellent ground cover in both shady or woodland gardens and sunny gravel and Mediterranean gardens; ideal for the wildlife garden; good in borders and in pots

FLOWERS June to September
SCENTED Aromatic leaves
ASPECT Any, in a sheltered or exposed position; full sun to partial shade
SOIL Any fertile, well-drained soil
HARDINESS Fully hardy at temperatures down to -15°C/5°F; needs no winter protection
DROUGHT TOLERANCE Excellent, once established
PROBLEMS Slugs, snails and vine weevil; powdery mildew
CARE Trim lightly after flowering, to encourage a second modest flowering
PROPAGATION Division in spring; sow seed in pots in a cold frame in spring

Helichrysum italicum
Curry plant

⬆ 60cm/24in ⬌ 80cm/32in   **EASY**

This dense, bushy, evergreen sub-shrub from the southern Mediterranean has small, narrow, silver grey leaves (3cm/1¼in long) that release their pungent spicy scent when bruised. The foliage whitens as the days grow hotter and drier, and offers a definite silvery presence throughout the year. Small, bobbly, mustard-coloured flower heads form upright flower sprays (8cm/3in across) from summer. *H.i.* subsp. *serotinum* (40cm/16in) is slightly more compact; *H.i.* 'Schwefellicht' (50cm/20in) has (to my mind) superior pale sulphur yellow flowers.

BEST USES Ideal for Mediterranean and gravel gardens and sunny borders; good in rock gardens and containers

FLOWERS July to September
SCENTED Aromatic leaves
ASPECT South, west or east facing, in a sheltered position with protection from cold winds; full sun
SOIL Any fertile, well-drained soil
HARDINESS Frost hardy at temperatures down to -5°C/23°F; may need winter protection
DROUGHT TOLERANCE Excellent, once established
PROBLEMS None
CARE Remove straggling stems and damaged growth in spring; if plant gets leggy, cut back hard in late spring, after all danger of frosts has passed
PROPAGATION Sow seed in pots in a cold frame in spring; semi-ripe cuttings in summer

Helictotrichon sempervirens 'Saphirsprudel' Blue oat grass

⬆ 90cm/3ft ⬌ 80cm/32in **EASY**

This clump-forming, architectural perennial evergreen grass from southern Europe is highly ornamental and looks handsome all year. It makes a fountaining, upright clump with gently arching grassy steely-grey leaves (20cm/8in long) and, like many grey-foliaged plants, the hot summer sun seems to heighten the colour. In summer, spiky, pale buff-coloured flower panicles (15cm/6in long) appear, held on slim, straight, blue-grey tall stems, and tremble charmingly when stirred by the breeze.

BEST USES Ideal for Mediterranean and gravel gardens; perfect for contemporary urban gardens and roof terraces; good for wildlife and prairie planting; great in containers

FLOWERS June to July; grown mainly for foliage
SCENTED No
ASPECT Any, in a sheltered or exposed position; full sun
SOIL Any fertile, moist, well-drained soil
HARDINESS Fully hardy at temperatures down to -15°C/5°F; needs no winter protection
DROUGHT TOLERANCE Good, once established
PROBLEMS Rust
CARE Rake out tatty leaves with your fingers in spring or as needed
PROPAGATION Self-seeds easily; division in spring; sow seed in pots in a cold frame in spring

Heuchera 'Persian Carpet' Coral bells

⬆ 55cm/22in ⬌ 30cm/12in **EASY**

This clump-forming, mounded, semi-evergreen hardy perennial from mountainous areas of North America has pronounced deeply lobed pinky purple veins running through ghostly silver leaves (10cm/4in long), which remain spectacular in mild winters. Slender, damson-coloured upright stems are studded with tiny, delicate, green-tan flowers along their length from early summer.

BEST USES Excellent border plant; good as edging; effective ground cover planted en masse

FLOWERS June to August
SCENTED No
ASPECT South, west or east facing, in a sheltered or exposed position; full sun to partial shade
SOIL Any fertile, humus-rich, well-drained soil; add organic matter before planting
HARDINESS Fully hardy at temperatures down to -15°C/5°F; needs no winter protection
DROUGHT TOLERANCE Good, once established
PROBLEMS None
CARE Cut back tatty foliage in early spring; mulch with organic matter around the crown in spring
PROPAGATION Division in spring or autumn; detach and pot up rooted plantlets in spring or early autumn

GREENFINGER TIP *Heucheras may rise up after frosts: check in spring and firm them back down*

Lavandula angustifolia 'Hidcote' ♊
English lavender

⬆ 60cm/24in ⬌ 75cm/30in **EASY**

This evergreen shrub from the Mediterranean makes compact mounds of aromatic, narrow, soft grey leaves (5cm/2in long) and has deeply scented deep blue flower spires (8cm/3in long), borne on narrow, upright silver stems. *L.a.* 'Loddon Pink' ♊ (45cm/18in tall) has pastel pink flowers; *L.a.* 'Nana Alba' ♊ (30cm/12in tall) has white flowers; *L.a.* 'Munstead' (45cm/18in tall) has deep violet spikes.

BEST USES Ideal for cottage, coastal and formal gardens; a must for Mediterranean and gravel gardens; good for edging paths or as a small, informal hedge; handy under shrub roses to clothe their naked lower limbs

FLOWERS July to September
SCENTED Scented flowers; aromatic foliage
ASPECT South, west or east facing, in a sheltered position; full sun
SOIL Any fertile, well-drained soil
HARDINESS Fully hardy at temperatures down to -15°C/5°F; needs no winter protection
DROUGHT TOLERANCE Excellent, once established
PROBLEMS Froghoppers; *Botrytis* (grey mould)
CARE Trim lightly in spring, taking care not to cut into the old wood; cut the flower stalks back after flowering to prevent plant becoming straggly
PROPAGATION Sow seed in pots in a cold frame in spring; semi-ripe cuttings in early summer

Libertia grandiflora ♊
New Zealand satin flower

⬆ 90cm/3ft ⬌ 90cm/3ft **EASY**

An upright, rhizomatous evergreen perennial from New Zealand, this makes handsome rounded clumps of leathery, sword-like, bright green leaves (30cm/12in long). It produces tall, long-lasting flower spikes of small, pure white flowers (3cm/1¼in across) with saffron yellow stamens; the flowers are iris-like in appearance and open from the bottom up from late spring. They are followed by pretty orange seed heads that ripen and split to reveal appealing shiny black seeds. It is borderline hardy, but there should be no problem growing it in frost-free areas.

BEST USES Excellent for prairie-planting, Mediterranean and gravel gardens, and in wildflower gardens; good cut or dried flower

FLOWERS May to July
SCENTED No
ASPECT South or west facing, in a sheltered position; full sun
SOIL Any fertile, well-drained soil; will struggle in heavy clay
HARDINESS Fully hardy/borderline at temperatures down to -15°C/5°F; may need winter protection in cold areas
DROUGHT TOLERANCE Excellent, once established
PROBLEMS None
CARE Cut back the flower spikes after flowering
PROPAGATION Self-seeds easily; division in spring

Ophiopogon planiscapus 'Nigrescens' ♡
Black lily turf

⬆ 20cm/8in ⬌ 30cm/12in   **MEDIUM**

This slow-growing Asian evergreen perennial makes small tufted hummocks and is admired for its slightly narrow, arching, purple-black grass-like leaves (30cm/12in long). It produces tiny, hanging bell-like flowers (6mm/¼in long) that are flushed purple and white in bud, opening to white petals with creamy stamens. Small clusters of rounded, blue-black berries follow the flowers, but are hard to spot against the dark foliage. Although slow to spread, it eventually makes good ground cover. *O.p.* 'Little Tabby' has variegated green leaves, striped silver.

BEST USES Plant in multiples for ground cover on slopes and banks or in coastal, gravel and Mediterranean gardens; good as edging at the front of sunny borders; works well in containers and pots in urban gardens or sunny patios

FLOWERS June to August; grown mainly for foliage
SCENTED No
ASPECT South, west or east facing, in a sheltered or exposed position; full sun to partial shade
SOIL Any fertile, well-drained soil; a slightly acid soil sees leaf colour at its best
HARDINESS Fully hardy at temperatures down to -15°C/5°F; needs no winter protection
DROUGHT TOLERANCE Excellent, once established
PROBLEMS Slugs and snails; slow to spread
CARE Remove any tatty leaves
PROPAGATION Division in spring

Pachysandra terminalis
Japanese spurge

⬆ 20cm/8in ⬌ Indefinite   **EASY**

This carpeting, evergreen perennial, native to Asia, has tough, leathery, oblong leaves (10cm/4in across), with toothed edges; the leaves overlap pleasingly, making dense ground cover. Rather ordinary small spikes of pure white, tubular flowers appear in spring, with male and female flowers on the same stem. It has a justified reputation for invasiveness. *P.t.* 'Green Carpet' ♡ (15cm/6in tall) is small and neat; *P.t.* 'Variegata' ♡ (20cm/8in) is slower-growing and less invasive.

BEST USES Excellent ground cover in a woodland garden and in damp or shady borders; ideal under trees and shrubs or clothing awkward slopes and banks; useful as edging

FLOWERS June; grown mainly for foliage
SCENTED No
ASPECT South, west or east facing, in a sheltered or exposed position; full sun to partial shade
SOIL Any fertile, humus-rich, well-drained soil; add organic matter before planting
HARDINESS Fully hardy at temperatures down to -15°C/5°F; needs no winter protection
DROUGHT TOLERANCE Good, once established
PROBLEMS None
CARE Cut back in spring or late summer to maintain desired size and spread
PROPAGATION Division in spring or autumn; semi-ripe cuttings in summer or autumn

Phlomis fruticosa 🎖
Jerusalem sage

⬆ 90cm/3ft ↔ 1.5m/5ft   **EASY**

This architectural, upright evergreen shrub hails
from the Mediterranean, so has a good drought
pedigree. It has aromatic, slightly coarse, felty,
sage-like grey-green leaves (10cm/4in long).
Come summer, curious hooded bright golden
yellow flowers (3cm/1¼in long) clasp the tall,
straight, slightly bristled stems at intervals, like
clinging golden rings. It is low maintenance, and
quickly makes a good-sized architectural plant,
so give it plenty of space when first planting.

BEST USES Excellent in the Mediterranean and
gravel garden, sunny border, cottage or wildlife
garden; ideal for coastal gardens

FLOWERS July to September
SCENTED Aromatic leaves
ASPECT South, west or east facing, in a sheltered
    position; full sun
SOIL Any fertile, well-drained soil
HARDINESS Fully hardy/borderline at temperatures
    down to -15°C/5°F; may need winter protection in
    cold areas
DROUGHT TOLERANCE Excellent, once established
PROBLEMS Leafhoppers
CARE In spring, cut back to the base of the plant any
    stems or foliage damaged by frosts
PROPAGATION Sow seed in pots in a greenhouse
    at minimum 13°C/55°F in spring; softwood cuttings
    in summer

Prostanthera cuneata 🎖
Mint bush

⬆ 90cm/3ft ↔ 90cm/3ft   **EASY**

This spreading, woody-based evergreen shrub
from Tasmania offers appealing mounded foliage
and pretty flowers. The tiny, shiny, rounded dark
green leaves (6mm/¼in long) give off a lovely
fresh minty aroma when bruised. Generous
numbers of pretty, small, tubular white-lipped
flowers, spotted with appealing purple freckles
inside the petals, form long flower clusters
(20cm/8in long). A handsome plant, it is hardier
than other species of its kind but really needs the
shelter of a warm wall to thrive. Or grow it in a
container that can be moved indoors when it
turns chilly and frosts threaten.

BEST USES Good in a Mediterranean garden or as
ground cover on a sheltered sunny bank; perfect for
'white' or coastal gardens

FLOWERS June to August
SCENTED Aromatic leaves
ASPECT South or west facing, in a sheltered position;
    full sun
SOIL Any fertile, well-drained soil
HARDINESS Frost hardy at temperatures down to
    -5°/23°F; may need winter protection
DROUGHT TOLERANCE Excellent, once established;
    will need watering if grown in pots
PROBLEMS Aphids (whitefly) and red spider mite,
    when grown indoors
CARE Trim lightly after flowering
PROPAGATION Semi-ripe cuttings in summer

Ruta graveolens 'Jackman's Blue'
Common rue

⬆ 60cm/24in ⬌ 75cm/30in　　　　**EASY**

This rounded, multi-stemmed, evergreen shrub from the Mediterranean is famed for its appealing foliage, with deeply cut, metallic, pungent, bitter-orange-scented blue-green leaves (15cm/6in long). It flowers in early summer, but the small sprays of dull, yellow flowers (2cm/¾in across) are not its best feature. I suggest you trim off the flowers and admire the foliage. The leaf colour is best when planted in full sun.

BEST USES Excellent ground cover for slopes and rockeries; ideal for coastal gardens; good in cottage gardens and in pots and containers in modern, urban gardens

FLOWERS June to September; grown mainly for foliage
SCENTED Aromatic leaves
ASPECT South, west or east facing, in a sheltered or exposed position; full sun
SOIL Any fertile, well-drained soil
HARDINESS Fully hardy at temperatures down to -15°C/5°F; needs no winter protection
DROUGHT TOLERANCE Excellent, once established
PROBLEMS Root rots
CARE Trim back to 2.5cm/1in above the old growth after flowering
PROPAGATION Sow seed in pots in a cold frame in spring; semi-ripe cuttings in summer

••

GREENFINGER TIP *Wear gloves when taking cuttings as the leaves can cause skin irritation*

Sagina subulata var. *glabrata* 'Aurea'
Pearlwort/Scotch moss

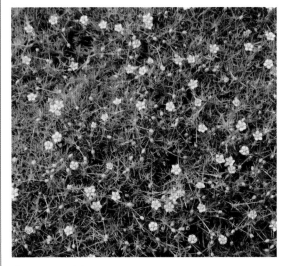

⬆ 1cm/⅜in ⬌ 20cm/8in+　　　　**MEDIUM**

This European carpeting evergreen perennial makes appealing, tight, dense mats of lime green foliage. The creeping stems have tiny, linear, zingy greeny yellow leaves (1cm/⅜in long), forming dense, springy mounds of mossy webbing. In summer, short, slim light green stems bear simple, star-shaped, translucent white flowers (3mm/⅛in across), studding the mossy foliage like small sparkling jewels. The foliage continues to add a splash of brightness in winter. It can't cope with extreme heat, though likes full sun (with afternoon shade); it detests sitting in winter wet but can stand light foot traffic. Sharp drainage is the key to growing success.

BEST USES Ideal ground cover in dappled shade in woodland, Oriental or rock gardens; good between paving stones or clothing slopes and banks; good in pots and troughs; deer proof

FLOWERS June
SCENTED No
ASPECT Any, in a sheltered or exposed position; full sun to partial shade
SOIL Any fertile, well-drained soil
HARDINESS Fully hardy at temperatures down to -15°C/5°F; needs no winter protection
DROUGHT TOLERANCE Poor
PROBLEMS Aphids
CARE Deadhead after flowering to prevent self-seeding
PROPAGATION Division in spring; sow seed in pots in a cold frame in autumn

Salvia officinalis 'Icterina' ♀
Sage

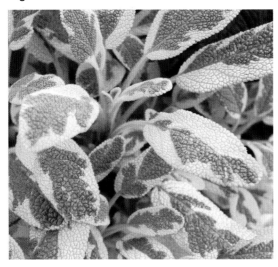

↑ 80cm/32in ↔ 90cm/3ft   **EASY**

This rounded, low-growing, evergreen perennial from the Mediterranean and North Africa has soft, felty, pointed, oval, aromatic sage green leaves (8cm/3in long), edged in paler gold-green. If it flowers, which it occasionally does, it produces branching spires of tubular, lipped, soft lilac-blue flowers (1.5cm/½in long) in summer. *S.o.* 'Tricolor' has grey-green leaves splashed purple and cream; *S.o.* 'Purpurascens' ♀ has mauve flowers and purple-flushed foliage.

BEST USES Invaluable in the herb, cottage or Mediterranean garden

FLOWERS June to August
SCENTED Aromatic leaves
ASPECT South, west or east facing, in a sheltered or exposed position; full sun
SOIL Any fertile, well-drained soil
HARDINESS Fully hardy at temperatures down to -15°C/5°F; needs no winter protection
DROUGHT TOLERANCE Excellent, once established
PROBLEMS Slugs and snails like to nibble the young foliage
CARE Prune very lightly after flowering (if there are any flowers)
PROPAGATION Softwood cuttings in late spring; semi-ripe cuttings in a heated propagator in late summer

Santolina pinnata subsp. *neapolitana* ♀
Cotton lavender

↑ 75cm/30in ↔ 90cm/3ft   **EASY**

This bushy, rounded, evergreen shrub from Italy has finely serrated silver grey leaves (4cm/1½in long), which give off a strong camphorous scent when crushed. In summer, it is smothered in small, button-like pale yellow flowers (2cm/¾in across), which you can shear off to make the most of the foliage. *S.p.* subsp. 'Edward Bowles' (80cm/32in) has creamy white flowers.

BEST USES Ideal ground cover in gravel, Mediterranean, cottage and rock gardens; excellent as low hedging; makes compact topiary

FLOWERS June
SCENTED Aromatic leaves
ASPECT South, west or east facing, in a sheltered position; full sun
SOIL Any fertile, well-drained soil
HARDINESS Frost hardy at temperatures down to -5°C/23°F; may need winter protection
DROUGHT TOLERANCE Excellent, once established
PROBLEMS None
CARE Cut back flowered stems to 2.5cm/1in above old growth, after flowering or in spring
PROPAGATION Sow seed in pots in a cold frame in spring or autumn; semi-ripe cuttings in a heated propagator in summer

GREENFINGER TIP *For tight, compact growth, cut off the flower heads after flowering and then cut back again (as described above) in March*

Saxifraga 'Kinki Purple'
Saxifrage

↑ 30cm/12in ↔ 90cm/3ft   **EASY**

This alpine saxifrage is a carpeting, rhizomatous evergreen perennial, found in mountainous areas across Japan. It makes gorgeous deep purple carpets from rounded, slightly overlapping, veined deep purple leaves (9cm/3½in long). Plum-coloured branching flower stems carry tiny, delicate white flowers (8mm/³/₈in across) that look both dainty and pleasing, held high above the dark scallops of moody foliage in summer. S. 'Tricolor' ♈ has mid-green, scalloped leaves with creamy veining and speckled pink edges.

> **BEST USES** Excellent camouflage for rock gardens and on well-drained slopes and banks; ideal at the front of borders and in pots or containers; good for woodland and shady garden corners as long as the soil is reliably free-draining

FLOWERS June to September
SCENTED No
ASPECT South, west or east facing, in a sheltered or exposed position; partial shade
SOIL Any fertile, moist, well-drained soil
HARDINESS Frost hardy at temperatures down to -5°C/23°F; may need winter protection
DROUGHT TOLERANCE Poor
PROBLEMS Aphids, slugs, snails and vine weevil
CARE Remove spent flower stems; protect from frosts
PROPAGATION Division in spring; dig up rooted mini-rosettes and pot up in late spring

Sedum spurium 'Schorbuser Blut' ♈
Crimson stonecrop

↑ 10cm/4in ↔ 60cm/24in   **EASY**

This low-growing, mat-forming evergreen perennial from Iran has succulent rosettes of rounded, pale green leaves (2.5cm/1in long), with spreading, fleshy, red-tinted stems holding low-rise flower clusters (4cm/1½in across), composed of a myriad of tiny star-shaped deep pink flowers. S.p. 'Ruby Mantle' has red-pink-flushed foliage; S.p. 'Fuldaglut' has green leaves flushed red; S.p. 'Voodoo' has eye-catching deep burgundy foliage.

> **BEST USES** Excellent ground cover in gravel, rock, Mediterranean or cottage gardens; good draped over low stone walls

FLOWERS August
SCENTED No
ASPECT South or west facing, in a sheltered position; full sun
SOIL Any fertile, humus-rich, well-drained soil
HARDINESS Fully hardy at temperatures down to -15°C/5°F; needs no winter protection
DROUGHT TOLERANCE Excellent, once established
PROBLEMS Slugs and snails
CARE Trim lightly after flowering
PROPAGATION Division in spring

GREENFINGER TIP Pull away small stems from the base and pot them up in gritty compost: hey presto, you have new plants

Teucrium fruticans 'Azureum' ♉
Shrubby germander

⬆ 90cm/3ft ⬌ 1.5m/5ft   **EASY**

This bushy Mediterranean evergreen shrub has long, arching stems clothed in aromatic, small, oval, silvery sage green leaves with white felty undersides (2cm/¾in long); planting it in full sun heightens the leaf colour. Small but plentiful tubular, droopy-lipped pale blue flowers, about the same size as the leaves, with silver white antennae-like stamens, smother the plant for a good four months from summer to early autumn.

> **BEST USES** Ideal in coastal, Mediterranean, gravel and cottage gardens; excellent for rock gardens; good as edging; useful in window boxes, pots and containers; good planted with white, mauve, pink and yellow flowers

FLOWERS June to September
SCENTED Aromatic leaves
ASPECT South, west or east facing, in a sheltered position; full sun to partial shade
SOIL Any fertile or poor, well-drained soil
HARDINESS Frost hardy at temperatures down to -5°C/23°F; may need winter protection
DROUGHT TOLERANCE Excellent, once established
PROBLEMS None
CARE In early spring, cut back to new growth at the base of the plant
PROPAGATION Softwood cuttings in a heated propagator in early summer; semi-ripe cuttings in a heated propagator in mid-summer

Thymus serpyllum 'Pink Chintz' ♉
Thyme

⬆ 25cm/10in ⬌ 45cm/18in   **EASY**

Thymes are carpeting evergreen shrubs famed for their aromatic foliage. This small, tidy, creeping European shrublet has trailing stems, densely clothed in tiny, oval, dark grey-green leaves (8mm/³⁄₈in long at best). In summer, tiny pale pink flowers smother the stems, attracting every bee for miles. *T.s.* 'Goldstream' has emerald and gold variegated leaves, with pale lilac flowers; *T.s.* 'Snowdrift' has white flowers.

> **BEST USES** Ideal for pots or the herb garden; good as edging; ideal ground cover in a gravel or Mediterranean garden; good between paving stones or covering stone walls and rockeries

FLOWERS June to July
SCENTED Aromatic leaves
ASPECT South, west or east facing, in a sheltered position; full sun
SOIL Any fertile, well-drained soil, especially neutral to alkaline soils
HARDINESS Fully hardy at temperatures down to -15°C/5°F; needs no winter protection
DROUGHT TOLERANCE Excellent, once established
PROBLEMS None
CARE Trim lightly after flowering to keep growth bushy
PROPAGATION Division in spring; softwood cuttings in early summer; semi-ripe cuttings in late summer

GREENFINGER TIP *If growing as ground cover, mow lightly after flowering, with the blades set high*

Abelia x grandiflora

⬆ 3m/10ft ↔ 4m/13ft   **EASY**

This rounded fully or semi-evergreen shrub of garden origin has slightly arching branches, densely clothed with oval, polished deep green leaves (5cm/2in long) that are flushed orange in mild winters. The pliable red stems bear a profusion of pink buds that open to masses of sweetly scented, tubular pinky white flowers, about half the size of the leaves, from summer into autumn.

> **BEST USES** Useful as evergreen hedging; ideal for the mixed shrub or perennial border; good in cottage and informal gardens; a lure for bees

FLOWERS July to October
SCENTED Scented flowers
ASPECT South or west facing, in a sheltered position; full sun
SOIL Any fertile, moist, well-drained soil
HARDINESS Frost hardy at temperatures down to -5°C/23°F; may need winter protection
DROUGHT TOLERANCE Poor
PROBLEMS None
CARE Deadhead to prolong flowering; in autumn, after final flowering, lightly trim back any flowering shoots to maintain size and shape
PROPAGATION Semi-ripe cuttings in late summer

••

GREENFINGER TIP *After a few years, cut back some of the older growth to ground level, to keep the shrub producing good flower displays*

Atriplex halimus
Tree purslane

⬆ 2m/6ft ↔ 2m/6ft   **EASY**

This southern European semi-evergreen shrub is a fast-growing, upright, spreading bush with a free and easy temperament and, in my experience, great foliage all year round. It has pale green stems, clothed in interesting diamond-shaped silver grey leaves (6cm/2½in long) and tiny greeny white flowers in summer; the flowers are so insignificant that you'll hardly notice it's in flower, which confirms its status as an outstanding foliage plant. This is a shrub that can survive punishing salt spray and drought equally well. I can't recommend it highly enough.

> **BEST USES** Useful as evergreen hedging for seaside gardeners or as a feature shrub; ideal for the Mediterranean, dry or gravel garden in a hot, sunny spot

FLOWERS July; grown mainly for foliage
SCENTED No
ASPECT South or west facing, in a sheltered position with protection from cold winds; full sun
SOIL Any fertile, well-drained soil
HARDINESS Frost hardy at temperatures down to -5°C/23°F; may need winter protection
DROUGHT TOLERANCE Excellent, once established
PROBLEMS None
CARE Remove dead, diseased or damaged material in late winter or early spring
PROPAGATION Softwood cuttings in summer

Azara serrata

⬆ 4m/13ft ↔ 3m/10ft   **EASY**

This upright, evergreen shrub from Chile has a slightly unruly habit, with lightly arching pinkish stems carrying lightly serrated, oval, polished deep green leaves (6cm/2½in long). It bears prolific clusters of small, fruity-scented, rich golden yellow blossoms (2cm/¾in across). Round white berries are sometimes, though not reliably, produced after a long hot summer. It is probably best planted against a warm sunny wall.

BEST USES A lovely plant for cottage and formal gardens alike; ideal for adding evergreen bones and a splash of colour to a shady city garden; can be trained as a wall shrub

FLOWERS June to July
SCENTED Scented flowers
ASPECT South, west or east facing, in a sheltered position; full sun to partial shade
SOIL Any fertile, well-drained soil
HARDINESS Frost hardy at temperatures down to -5°C/23°F; may need winter protection
DROUGHT TOLERANCE Good, once established
PROBLEMS None; late frosts can damage the flowers
CARE Prune lightly after flowering; if grown as a wall shrub, cut back flowered shoots after flowering, in late winter or early spring, to maintain size and shape
PROPAGATION Semi-ripe cuttings in summer

Berberidopsis corallina
Coral plant

⬆ 4m/13ft ↔ 2m/6ft   **TRICKY**

This South American twining evergreen climber is among my top ten climbers, although it is high maintenance. It has dense, oval, slightly saw-edged, shiny deep green leaves, which are elegant throughout the year. Clustered bunches of small, baubled, deep rich red flowers (1cm/³⁄₈in across) hang festively from waxy-looking red stems from summer to autumn. Of course you pay the price for such beauty: this is slow to establish and needs pretty exacting conditions. If you can offer a suitably acid soil and throw in some extra nurturing, it will thrive.

BEST USES An exotic climber for sheltered beds, or in pots and containers on sheltered patios and courtyards

FLOWERS July to September
SCENTED No
ASPECT West or east facing, in a sheltered position with protection from cold winds; partial shade; needs cool, humid conditions
SOIL Any fertile, moist, humus-rich, well-drained acid soil
HARDINESS Frost hardy at temperatures down to -5°C/23°F; may need winter protection
DROUGHT TOLERANCE Poor
PROBLEMS Aphids
CARE Remove dead, diseased or damaged material in early spring
PROPAGATION Softwood cuttings in a heated propagator in spring

Bupleurum fruticosum
Shrubby hare's ear

⬆ 2m/6ft ⬌ 2.5m/8ft   **EASY**

This dense, rounded Mediterranean evergreen shrub is fairly quick-growing and has attractive, small, oval, blue-green leaves (8cm/3in long). The foliage is thick and plentiful, making it an ideal topiary plant. In summer, it is covered in umbrella-like domes (4cm/1½in across) comprised of tiny, starry, acid yellow flowers that attract hoverflies and other insects. It will take any soil but waterlogged and should come through harsh winters if given protection.

BEST USES Excellent as hedging for seaside gardens; good as a focal plant for gravel, Mediterranean and cottage gardens; ideal for topiary and in pots and containers

FLOWERS July to September
SCENTED No
ASPECT South or west facing, in a sheltered position; full sun to partial shade
SOIL Any fertile, well-drained soil
HARDINESS Fully hardy/borderline at temperatures down to -15°C/5°F; may need winter protection in cold areas
DROUGHT TOLERANCE Good, once established
PROBLEMS None
CARE Trim lightly in early spring
PROPAGATION Semi-ripe cuttings in late summer

GREENFINGER TIP *If your plant looks straggly, cut it down to ground level to get it thriving again*

Carpenteria californica ⚕
Tree anemone

⬆ 2m/6ft ⬌ 2m/6ft   **EASY**

This lovely upright, open, evergreen shrub from California has peeling bark, resembling cinnamon curls, and leathery, oval, highly polished green leaves (13cm/5in long), tapering to a point. The sweetly fragrant, shallow, bowl-like flowers have overlapping white petals (4–8cm/1½–3in across), with bright golden centres made up of pollen-dusty golden stamens. Plant in a sunny border, or against a warm wall. *C.c.* 'Ladhams' Variety' has slightly larger gappy white flowers.

BEST USES Excellent for Mediterranean and cottage gardens; good in large pots in a courtyard

FLOWERS June to July
SCENTED Scented flowers
ASPECT South or west facing, in a sheltered position with protection from strong winds; full sun
SOIL Any fertile, moist, well-drained soil
HARDINESS Frost hardy at temperatures down to -5°C/23°F; may need winter protection
DROUGHT TOLERANCE Good, once established
PROBLEMS Leaf spot
CARE Trim lightly after flowering
PROPAGATION Sow seed in pots in a greenhouse at 13–18°C/55–64°F in spring or autumn; semi-ripe cuttings in summer

GREENFINGER TIP *It is normal for older leaves to yellow at the end of summer, and cold winters can cause some leaf loss*

Cassinia fulvida
Golden heather

↑ 2m/6ft ↔ 2.5m/8ft   **EASY**

A sun-loving New Zealander found in scrub and grassland in its homeland, this makes a dependable, rather charmingly informal, tough, rounded, bushy, upright evergreen shrub. In its native country it is regarded as a nuisance, but our colder climate keeps it in check and it undoubtedly has its uses. The sticky, yellow-tinged stems are clothed in attractive small, narrow, linear dark green leaves (8mm/³⁄₈in long), with bristly yellow undersides. Tiny trumpet-shaped white flowers form domed, fragrant clusters (8cm/3in across) in summer.

BEST USES Excellent for the Mediterranean, gravel and cottage garden alike; good for clothing sunny slopes and banks in coastal gardens

FLOWERS June to July
SCENTED Scented flowers
ASPECT South or west facing, in a sheltered position with protection from strong winds; full sun
SOIL Any fertile, moist, well-drained soil
HARDINESS Fully hardy at temperatures down to -15°C/5°F; needs no winter protection
DROUGHT TOLERANCE Excellent, once established
PROBLEMS None
CARE Trim flowering shoots back to within 2.5cm/1in of older growth after flowering, to maintain size and shape
PROPAGATION Semi-ripe cuttings in summer

Ceanothus 'Autumnal Blue' ♻
Californian lilac

↑ 3m/10ft ↔ 3m/10ft   **EASY**

Californian lilacs are evergreen shrubs from California that can be grown free-standing or as wall shrubs. This fairly upright species has smart, glossy, delicately toothed, dark green leaves (5cm/2in long) and is smothered in clustered panicles of rich, azure blue and pure dark blue flowers (8cm/3in long) from late summer well into autumn. Ceanothus are low maintenance, relatively problem-free and reliable flowerers. C. 'Blue Mound' ♻ (1.5m/5ft) is more compact, with bright blue flowers in May; C. 'Concha' ♻ has dark blue flowers in May.

BEST USES Excellent against a warm sunny fence or wall; ideal for the Mediterranean, cottage, coastal or wildlife garden; good in pots

FLOWERS August to October
SCENTED No
ASPECT South, west or east facing, in a sheltered position with protection from cold winds; full sun
SOIL Any fertile, well-drained soil
HARDINESS Fully hardy at temperatures down to -15°C/5°F; needs no winter protection
DROUGHT TOLERANCE Excellent, once established
PROBLEMS Honey fungus
CARE Trim lightly after flowering, to maintain spread and size
PROPAGATION Semi-ripe cuttings in summer to autumn; sow seed in pots in a cold frame in autumn

Cortaderia selloana 'Pumila' 🎖
Pampas grass

⬆ 1.5m/5ft ⬌ 1.2m/4ft　　　　**EASY**

This architectural, clump-forming evergreen perennial grass has very tough, long, arching, narrow, razor-edged, mid-green grass-like leaves (2m/6ft or more long). Tall, erect, straw-coloured flower plumes are sent up in summer from the cascading grassy base, and can reach 2.5m/8ft. Pampas grass has been out of favour for many years, but I detect a resurgence in its popularity.

BEST USES Fantastic for wildlife or prairie planting schemes and Mediterranean or gravel gardens; a striking focal point in a large pot; birds like to nest in it; ideal dried flower

FLOWERS August

SCENTED No

ASPECT South, west or east facing, in a sheltered or exposed position; full sun

SOIL Any fertile, well-drained soil

HARDINESS Fully hardy at temperatures down to -15°C/5°F; needs no winter protection

DROUGHT TOLERANCE Excellent, once established

PROBLEMS None

CARE Cut out spent flower stems and dead growth from the base in winter; comb through by hand (wearing thick gloves to prevent cuts)

PROPAGATION Division in spring

GREENFINGER TIP *Division is a two-man job and moving a mature plant takes some digging, so site it carefully in the first place*

Desfontainia spinosa 🎖

⬆ 2m/6ft ⬌ 2m/6ft　　　　**MEDIUM**

Hailing from the South American Andes, this mounding, dense, evergreen shrub grows at a reasonable pace, with prickly, holly-like, deep green leaves (6cm/2½in long) which make it a very attractive foliage plant. In addition, it has exotic, waxy, drooping, tubular, vibrant flame red flowers (4cm/1½in long), tipped with canary yellow. It isn't frost proof by any means, but should come through winter easily enough in a sheltered spot in warmer regions.

BEST USES Ideal against a warm wall in an exotic or hot-coloured border; good in a woodland garden (where it gets shade and shelter); does well in pots

FLOWERS August to October

SCENTED No

ASPECT South, west or east facing, in a sheltered position with protection from strong winds; partial shade

SOIL Any fertile, moist, well-drained acid soil

HARDINESS Frost hardy at temperatures down to -5°C/23°F; may need winter protection

DROUGHT TOLERANCE Poor

PROBLEMS None

CARE Prune any unwanted growth lightly in spring

PROPAGATION Semi-ripe cuttings in summer

Escallonia 'Apple Blossom' 🎖

⬆ 2.5m/8ft ⬌ 2.5m/8ft   **EASY**

This compact, dense, bushy, evergreen shrub of South American origin has a strong growth habit and is thickly clothed in aromatic, small, oval, highly polished, deep green leaves (7cm/2¾in long) that smell resinous in wet weather. Generous clusters of rosy pink flower buds open to simple, star-shaped, apple blossom-like pale pinky white flowers (2.5cm/1in across). *E.* 'Donard Seedling' has white flowers flushed pink and is fast-growing.

BEST USES Perfect for cottage, formal, Mediterranean and coastal gardens; ideal as a small hedge or dwarf screen/windbreak; good for large pots and containers in sunny city courtyards

FLOWERS June to September
SCENTED Aromatic leaves
ASPECT Any, in a sheltered or exposed position; full sun
SOIL Any fertile, well-drained soil
HARDINESS Frost hardy at temperatures down to -5°C/23°F; may need winter protection
DROUGHT TOLERANCE Excellent, once established
PROBLEMS None
CARE Minimal pruning; remove any unwanted growth after flowering
PROPAGATION Softwood cuttings in early summer; semi-ripe cuttings in late summer; hardwood cuttings in late autumn to winter

GREENFINGER TIP *If it grows leggy, cut it back hard in spring to promote growth from the base*

Euphorbia mellifera 🎖
Honey spurge

⬆ 2m/6ft ⬌ 2.5m/8ft   **EASY**

This architectural evergreen shrub from Madeira is a superior foliage plant in every way. It makes a neat, rounded shape, clothed in narrow, pointed, deep green leaves (20cm/8in long), edged in pink, with a central creamy vein, on tall, upright stems. Tiny, honey-scented green and brown flowers form appealing fist-sized domes, which pollinating insects find madly attractive. It is fairly hardy in our climate, though will probably need protection in cold regions.

BEST USES Excellent architectural plant in the Mediterranean, gravel or wildlife garden; good for informal garden divisions; goat and deer proof

FLOWERS May to June
SCENTED Scented flowers
ASPECT South, west or east facing, in a sheltered position; full sun
SOIL Any fertile, moist, well-drained soil
HARDINESS Frost hardy at temperatures down to -5°C/23°F; may need winter protection
DROUGHT TOLERANCE Excellent, once established
PROBLEMS None
CARE Remove spent flower heads after flowering; take care not to cut into new growth
PROPAGATION Division in early spring; basal stem cuttings in early summer

GREENFINGER TIP *Euphorbias exude a milky sap when cut, which can cause skin irritation, so be sure to wear gloves when handling them*

Fabiana imbricata f. *violacea* 🎖
Violet pichi

⬆ 2.5m/8ft ↔ 2.5m/8ft — **EASY**

This striking evergreen shrub from Chile is rarely seen, but it is a very attractive foliage plant. Related to the potato family, it makes a mounded shape, with upright, slightly arching boughs, covered in dense, dark green needle-like foliage (up to 6mm/¼in long). In early summer, small, tubular, pale lavender-coloured flowers (1.5cm/½in long), with golden centres, decorate the slightly drooping, yellow-tipped fresh green stems in fair profusion, followed by small, pale green pea pods in autumn.

BEST USES Excellent as an architectural plant in the Mediterranean or gravel garden; good for the wildlife garden, as bees love it; grows well against a sunny wall

FLOWERS July
SCENTED No
ASPECT South or west facing, in a sheltered position with protection from cold winds; full sun
SOIL Any fertile, well-drained soil
HARDINESS Frost hardy at temperatures down to -5°C/23°F; may need winter protection
DROUGHT TOLERANCE Excellent, once established
PROBLEMS None
CARE Remove dead, diseased or damaged growth in spring
PROPAGATION Semi-ripe cuttings in late summer

Hypericum 'Hidcote' 🎖
St John's wort

⬆ 1.2m/4ft ↔ 1.5m/5ft — **EASY**

This domed, bushy, fully to semi-evergreen shrub from Asia is densely clothed in oval, deep green leaves (6cm/2½in long). The large, cupped, golden flowers, roughly the same size as the leaves, with pronounced golden stamens, are generous in number and really stand out against the dark foliage. It does well in most situations and needs little attention (although all hypericums are rust-prone).

BEST USES Excellent for Mediterranean, gravel or cottage gardens; grows well against a sunny wall or in containers as a wall shrub; useful ground cover on awkward banks and slopes; ideal for wildlife gardens

FLOWERS July to October
SCENTED No
ASPECT Any, in a sheltered or exposed position; full sun to partial shade (flowering is more profuse in full sun)
SOIL Any fertile, well-drained soil
HARDINESS Fully hardy at temperatures down to -15°C/5°F; needs no winter protection
DROUGHT TOLERANCE Excellent, once established
PROBLEMS Rust
CARE Low maintenance; prune lightly after flowering
PROPAGATION Semi-ripe cuttings in summer

GREENFINGER TIP *It will drop some leaves each year, with more severe loss in harsh winters*

Kalmia latifolia ♀
Calico bush

⬆ 3m/10ft ⬌ 3m/10ft   **EASY**

This bushy, rounded, free-flowering evergreen shrub from the USA is thickly clothed in elegant, elliptical, shiny, deep green leaves (10cm/4in long). From late spring into summer, bunched clusters of individual, cupped, pale to dark pink flowers (2.5cm/1in across), with raspberry ringing at the bases of the petals and radiating spider-like stamens, are borne in such joyful profusion at the stem tips that the branches arch downward under their weight. Acid soil is essential. *K.l.* 'Carousel' has white flowers with deep red freckles; *K.l.* 'Freckles' ♀ has cinnamon-spotted pale pinky white flowers.

> **BEST USES** Excellent for the woodland garden or shady border; ideal for both formal and informal gardens; good in pots and containers

FLOWERS May to July

SCENTED No

ASPECT North, east or west facing, in a sheltered or exposed position; full sun to partial shade

SOIL Any fertile, moist, humus-rich, well-drained acid soil

HARDINESS Fully hardy at temperatures down to -15°C/5°F; needs no winter protection

DROUGHT TOLERANCE Poor

PROBLEMS None

CARE Minimal; prune lightly after flowering to maintain size and shape

PROPAGATION Semi-ripe cuttings in mid-summer; layering in late summer

Kniphofia uvaria
Red hot poker

⬆ 2m/6ft ⬌ 90cm/3ft   **EASY**

This architectural, clump-forming evergreen perennial from South Africa has arching, linear, grass-like mid-green foliage (60cm/24in long). In summer, tall, sturdy, straight, upright stems are topped with flame-coloured, torch-like flowers (4cm/1½in long) that are deep red in bud, opening to orange, with fading pale lemon bases. It copes well with our climate, despite its exotic looks. Some kniphofias are not evergreen; others that are include *K.* 'Atlanta' (1.2m/4ft), with orange/red torches, and *K. caulescens* ♀ (1.2m/4ft), with red/yellow pokers.

> **BEST USES** Excellent for Mediterranean and gravel gardens, or exotic planting schemes; good for coastal and cottage gardens alike; perfect for wildlife gardens as they are irresistible to bees

FLOWERS July to September

SCENTED No

ASPECT South or west facing, in a sheltered or exposed position; full sun to partial shade (flowering is reduced in shade)

SOIL Any fertile, moist, well-drained soil

HARDINESS Fully hardy at temperatures down to -15°C/5°F; needs no winter protection

DROUGHT TOLERANCE Good, once established

PROBLEMS None

CARE Mulch young plants with organic matter in their first winter, and mulch annually in spring; cut back after flowering

PROPAGATION Division in spring

Lapageria rosea
Chilean bellflower

⬆ 4m/13ft ⬌ 2.5m/8ft   **EASY**

This twining, suckering, evergreen climber from Chile is fairly slow-growing, with oval, waxy, dark green leaves (13cm/5in long). It produces striking pendulous, gently flaring, bell-shaped rose pink flowers (9cm/3½in long), from summer into autumn. It looks too exotic to cope with cold, but does well in a sheltered, predominantly frost-free spot; try planting it against a sheltered north-facing wall.

> **BEST USES** Excellent trained up trellis, pillars, pergolas or obelisks; good in containers in a shady city courtyard

FLOWERS July to September
SCENTED No
ASPECT North, east or west facing, in a sheltered position; partial to full shade
SOIL Any fertile, well-drained soil; will not tolerate wet, heavy clay
HARDINESS Frost hardy at temperatures down to -5°C/23°F; may need winter protection
DROUGHT TOLERANCE Poor
PROBLEMS Aphids, mealybug and scale insect; cold winds can cause leaf loss or damage which prevents the plant establishing
CARE Trim lightly after flowering (if needed), to maintain size and shape
PROPAGATION Sow pre-soaked seed in pots in a greenhouse at 13–18°C/55–64°F in spring; semi-ripe cuttings in late summer; layering in autumn

Ligustrum japonicum 'Rotundifolium'
Japanese privet

⬆ 1.5m/5ft ⬌ 90cm/3ft   **EASY**

The privet family includes a number of very useful, handsome shrubs that make great focal plants or perform well as hedging and screening, but don't confuse this bushy, upright, slow-growing, Japanese evergreen shrub with the small-leaved common privet, usually associated with suburban hedging. This one has leathery, shiny, rounded olive green leaves (10cm/4in long) and produces long, musty-smelling white flower sprays in late summer, followed by rounded black berries.

> **BEST USES** Marvellous for hedges and screens; good for clothing banks or in shady corners; ideal in woodland, cottage or wildlife gardens

FLOWERS July to September
SCENTED Scented flowers
ASPECT Any, in a sheltered or exposed position; full sun to partial shade
SOIL Any fertile, moist, well-drained soil
HARDINESS Fully hardy/borderline at temperatures down to -15°C/5°F; may need winter protection in cold areas
DROUGHT TOLERANCE Excellent, once established
PROBLEMS Aphids and leaf miners; *Botrytis* (grey mould), honey fungus and leaf spot
CARE Clip hedges from early summer to early autumn; if growing as a single shrub, remove any unwanted stems in summer
PROPAGATION Semi-ripe cuttings in summer; hardwood cuttings in winter

Myrtus communis 🎖
Common myrtle

⬆ 3m/10ft ↔ 3m/10ft   **EASY**

This upright, bushy, evergreen shrub from the Mediterranean has oval, polished, deep green, aromatic leaves (5cm/2in long) that release a spicy orange scent when crushed. Fat, rounded, sweetly scented flower buds open to flat, saucer-shaped white flowers (2cm/¾in across), with exaggerated white stamens, so that the shrub looks as if it is studded with silken pom-poms from summer into autumn. Green berries, present as the flowers fade, mature to purple-black. It will grow best against a sunny wall or fence. *M.c.* 'Flore Pleno' has double white flowers.

BEST USES Excellent for cottage, formal, coastal or Mediterranean gardens; good for large pots and containers in sunny city gardens

FLOWERS July to August
SCENTED Scented flowers; aromatic leaves
ASPECT South or west facing, in a sheltered position; full sun
SOIL Any fertile, moist, well-drained soil
HARDINESS Frost hardy at temperatures down to -5°C/23°F; may need winter protection
DROUGHT TOLERANCE Excellent, once established
PROBLEMS None
CARE Remove dead, diseased or damaged material in late spring (after all frost risk has passed); if grown as a wall shrub, prune lightly after flowering
PROPAGATION Semi-ripe cuttings in a heated propagator in late summer

Ozothamnus rosmarinifolius
Sea rosemary

⬆ 3m/10ft ↔ 1.5m/5ft   **EASY**

This evergreen shrub from Tasmania is easily mistaken for rosemary; it has a similar upright, bushy habit, and the deep green needle-like leaves (4cm/1½in long), with silver white undersides, are almost identical, but the flowers are the giveaway: slender, branching stems hold a clutch of tiny pink-tinged flower buds that open to fragrant white flowers. These form branching, slightly domed flower heads (5cm/2in across) that last through summer, often up until the first frosts bite. *O.r.* 'Silver Jubilee' 🎖 has silvery foliage.

BEST USES Excellent ground cover in a gravel or Mediterranean garden; perfect for a sunny border or in containers

FLOWERS July to August (often up till first frosts)
SCENTED Scented flowers
ASPECT South or west facing, in a sheltered position; full sun
SOIL Any fertile, well-drained soil
HARDINESS Frost hardy at temperatures down to -5°C/23°F; may need winter protection
DROUGHT TOLERANCE Excellent, once established
PROBLEMS None
CARE Trim lightly after flowering, to maintain size and shape
PROPAGATION Semi-ripe cuttings in summer

GREENFINGER TIP *Always take a few cuttings, just in case this succumbs to the cold*

Phormium 'Yellow Wave' 🎖
New Zealand flax

⬆ 4m/13ft ⬌ 2m/6ft   **EASY**

This clump-forming evergreen perennial is a
tough, architectural New Zealander and is a
fairly quick grower. A multitude of flat, strappy,
leathery, upright, slightly arching yellow leaves
(90cm/3ft long), with mid-green striping, erupt
from the base of the plant. Sturdy, rigid, upright,
smooth, smoky-coloured stems produce sparse,
muted red flowers (5cm/2in long) in summer.
P. 'Apricot Queen' has dark green leaves with
ruby-chard-coloured margins; *P.* 'Dazzler' has
red and pink striped foliage.

> **BEST USES** Ideal for coastal gardens, and
> Mediterranean or gravel gardens; adds architectural
> form to the border all year round

FLOWERS July; grown mainly for foliage
SCENTED No
ASPECT Any, in a sheltered or exposed position; full sun
   to partial shade (foliage colours best in full sun)
SOIL Any fertile, well-drained soil
HARDINESS Fully hardy/borderline at temperatures
   down to -15°C/5°F; may need winter protection in
   cold areas
DROUGHT TOLERANCE Excellent, once established
PROBLEMS Mealybugs
CARE Cut out faded flower spikes and dead growth
   in spring
PROPAGATION Division in spring; sow seed in pots in
   a greenhouse at 18°C/64°F in spring

Yucca gloriosa 🎖
Spanish dagger

⬆ 2m/6ft ⬌ 2m/6ft   **EASY**

This large, upright, architectural evergreen shrub
from Florida has stout, woody stems with long,
sharply pointed, rigid, linear, bladed blue-green
leaves (60cm/24in long) that mature to deep
green. Small, bell-shaped, whitish-cream flowers,
which are often red-tinged, form large egg-
shaped flower spikes (2.5m/8ft long); these are
produced in isolated displays in late summer and
often into early autumn. The exotic-looking
foliage is striking – and fiercely injurious – all
year round. *Y.g.* 'Variegata' 🎖 has broad green-
blue leaves with creamy edges.

> **BEST USES** Excellent as a focal point in a gravel or
> Mediterranean garden; good for coastal gardens;
> does well in pots

FLOWERS August to September
SCENTED No
ASPECT South or west facing, in a sheltered position;
   full sun
SOIL Any well-drained soil
HARDINESS Frost hardy at temperatures down to
   -5°C/23°F; may need winter protection
DROUGHT TOLERANCE Excellent, once established
PROBLEMS Aphids; leaf spot
CARE Remove spent flower stems and any dead or
   damaged material as necessary
PROPAGATION Sow pre-soaked seed in pots in a
   heated greenhouse or propagator at 15°C/59°F in
   spring; detach and pot up rooted suckers in spring

Cordyline 'Red Star'
Cabbage palm

⬆ 7m/22ft ⬌ 3m/10ft   **EASY**

Cordylines are very sculptural evergreen palms from Australia and have tough, sinewy, sword-like, arching leaves of deep plum red (90cm/3ft long). They also have fragrant flowers: large upright flower spikes (90cm/3ft long), resembling mini white Christmas trees, are composed of densely packed clusters of very sweetly scented tubular creamy white flowers. Whitish berries often follow the flowers. C. Renegade (syn. C. 'Tana') (60cm/24in) has arching, moody purple-black leaves.

> **BEST USES** Excellent for a hot, sunny exotic border, or in Mediterranean and gravel gardens; ideal as focal points in large containers on city patios or roof terraces

FLOWERS July to August
SCENTED Scented flowers
ASPECT South or west facing, in a sheltered position; full sun to partial shade
SOIL Any fertile, well-drained soil
HARDINESS Frost hardy at temperatures down to -5°C/23°F; may need winter protection
DROUGHT TOLERANCE Excellent, once established
PROBLEMS None
CARE Mulch with organic matter in spring; remove any frost-damaged foliage once all risk of frost has passed
PROPAGATION Sow seed in pots in a heated greenhouse or propagator at 16°C/61°F in spring; detach and pot up rooted suckers in spring

Itea ilicifolia 🎖
Holly-leaf sweetspire

⬆ 5m/16ft ⬌ 3m/10ft   **MEDIUM**

This architectural, spreading evergreen shrub from China is densely clothed in highly polished, prickly-edged, holly-like dark green leaves (10cm/4in long). In summer, through to early autumn, it produces tiny, unremarkable, vanilla-scented greenish flowers (6mm/¼in across), which form elegant, catkin-like flower strings (30cm/12in long), giving the impression that the shrub is draped in tiered silken tassels. Slow-growing but dramatic, it can be grown as a free-standing shrub or, even better, as a wall shrub.

> **BEST USES** Excellent for a sunny border or wall; ideal as a focal point in a large pot on a city patio

FLOWERS July to September
SCENTED Scented flowers
ASPECT South or west facing, in a sheltered position with protection from cold winds; full sun to partial shade
SOIL Any fertile, moist, well-drained soil
HARDINESS Frost hardy at temperatures down to -5°C/23°F; may need winter protection
DROUGHT TOLERANCE Poor
PROBLEMS None
CARE Mulch young plants with organic matter in spring or autumn; remove dead, diseased or damaged wood in spring; trim wall-grown shrubs lightly after flowering, to maintain size and shape
PROPAGATION Semi-ripe cuttings in a heated propagator in summer; sow ripe seed immediately in pots in a cold frame

Magnolia grandiflora 'Samuel Sommer'

⬆ 6m/20ft ↔ 4m/13ft **EASY**

The evergreen magnolias resist drought, deer, rabbits, heat and humidity, and are spectacular formal, spreading, conical trees from the USA. This variety has a rounded habit, with narrow, glossy, deep green leaves (20cm/8in long), with typically rust-coloured undersides. The fragrant, lemon-scented, waxy, creamy white goblet-shaped flowers (35cm/14in across) are some of the largest among the evergreen species. *M.g.* 'Harold Poole' (4m/13ft) is more compact and shrubby but just as luxurious and seductive.

BEST USES Excellent as a focal point or wall shrub; good for screening in formal, coastal or cottage gardens; deer and rabbit proof

FLOWERS August to October

SCENTED Scented flowers

ASPECT Any, in a sheltered position with protection from strong winds; full sun to partial shade

SOIL Any fertile, well-drained soil

HARDINESS Fully hardy at temperatures down to -15°C/5°F; needs no winter protection

DROUGHT TOLERANCE Excellent, once established

PROBLEMS Scale insect; coral spot

CARE Remove dead, diseased or damaged wood in mid to late spring

PROPAGATION Semi-ripe cuttings in late summer to early autumn

Prunus lusitanica 🎖
Portuguese laurel

⬆ 20m/65ft ↔ 20m/65ft **EASY**

This upright, spreading, densely clothed evergreen shrub is a native of Spain and Portugal and makes an elegant, low-maintenance addition to the garden, providing year-round interest. It has a fairly rapid growth rate, with oval, deep dark green, glossy, leathery leaves (13cm/5in long), held on appealing, smooth, dark red stalks. In early summer, it bears long clusters of cup-shaped hawthorn-scented white flowers (1.5cm/½in across), followed by small rounded berries that ripen to black. *P.l.* 'Variegata' has dark green leaves with creamy edges.

BEST USES Ideal as a hedging or screening plant; perfect for the wildlife, woodland or cottage garden; good for topiary

FLOWERS June

SCENTED Scented flowers

ASPECT Any, in a sheltered or exposed position; full sun to partial shade

SOIL Any fertile, well-drained soil, including chalk

HARDINESS Fully hardy at temperatures down to -15°C/5°F; needs no winter protection

DROUGHT TOLERANCE Excellent, once established

PROBLEMS Vine weevil; powdery mildew and silver leaf

CARE Clip hedges once a year in summer, after flowering; clip topiary three times a year, in February, June and October

PROPAGATION Semi-ripe cuttings in a heated propagator in summer

AUTUMN

Laced with its tang of bonfires and mornings edged in chilly dampness, autumn pervades our gardens with gentle pace. A languorous tempo seems to overtake the last of the bees droning on the limey umbels of late-flowering ivies. Shrubs hang enticingly with chandeliered clusters of vivid flame- and wine-coloured berries, displaying their tasty wares to foraging birds.

Autumn-flowering evergreens give us an unexpected encore of colour, coupled with often intoxicating fragrance, as if signalling the foreclosure of the gardening year and encouraging us to make the most of our gardens while the weather remains mild.

Calluna vulgaris 'Annemarie' ᛦ
Heather

⬆ 50cm/20in ⬌ 60cm/24in   EASY

Heather grows wild on the moors and hillsides of the British Isles. This spreading, ground-hugging variety has trademark tiny dark green leaves (3mm/⅛in long), and produces short, upright stems (10cm/4in long), clustered with tiny bells of double, rose-pink flowers. As the plants age, their flowering spikes shorten in length. Very free-draining acid soil is the key to success; heathers can't bear clay soil or alkalinity. They are generally pink, mauve or white in colour, but *C.v.* 'Wickwar Flame' ᛦ has flame orange flowers and *C.v.* 'Red Pimpernel' has deep crimson flowers. *C.v.* 'Golden Turret' has golden greeny yellow foliage.

BEST USES Ideal ground cover, and for clothing slopes and banks; does well in coastal gardens; good for wildlife gardens; easy in pots

FLOWERS September to October
SCENTED No
ASPECT South, west or east facing, in a sheltered or exposed position; full sun
SOIL Any fertile, moist, well-drained acid soil
HARDINESS Fully hardy at temperatures down to -15°C/5°F; needs no winter protection
DROUGHT TOLERANCE Good, for brief spells only
PROBLEMS None
CARE Cut back flowered shoots to within 2.5cm/1in of the older growth
PROPAGATION Layering in spring; semi-ripe cuttings in summer

Danae racemosa
Alexandrian laurel/Poet's laurel

⬆ 90cm/3ft ⬌ 90cm/3ft   MEDIUM

This spreading, low-growing, clump-forming, shrubby evergreen perennial from Turkey is a handsome foliage plant. Pointed, tapering, shiny, dark green leaves (10cm/4in long) clothe arching green stems which bear tiny, baubled yellow-green flowers. These form pretty enough clusters (5cm/2in long), but it is the rounded, pea-sized, orangey red berries which follow after hot summers that really stand out. It looks a bit like a dense, low-growing bamboo, but is much more attractive, and tolerates shady or dry ground. It has a slowish growing rate.

BEST USES Useful for borders and as ground cover; performs well as an evergreen hedge, as it takes to clipping admirably

FLOWERS June; grown mainly for foliage and autumn berry display

SCENTED No

ASPECT Any, in a sheltered position; partial to full shade

SOIL Any fertile, well-drained soil; add organic matter before planting

HARDINESS Fully hardy at temperatures down to -15°C/5°F; needs no winter protection

DROUGHT TOLERANCE Excellent, once established

PROBLEMS None

CARE Prune dead or damaged stems back to ground level in spring

PROPAGATION Division in autumn; sow seed in pots in a cold frame in autumn

Farfugium japonicum 'Aureomaculatum' ♀ Leopard plant

⬆ 60cm/24in ⬌ 60cm/24in   MEDIUM

This clump-forming evergreen perennial from Japan and Korea has large, vein-etched, rounded, kidney-shaped, glossy deep green leaves (30cm/12in across), decorated with large splashes of conspicuous cream marbling; a few plants go a long way because of the size of the leaves. The flowers, kindly described as daisy-like, are tatty and brassy yellow, on unattractive buff-coloured stems; shear them off and enjoy the foliage. *F.j.* 'Crispatum' has felty pale green-tan crimped-edged leaves.

BEST USES Ideal ground cover in damp, shady gardens and by ponds and streams; useful in containers to brighten a gloomy city garden

FLOWERS October onwards; grown mainly for foliage

SCENTED No

ASPECT Any, in a sheltered position; partial to full shade

SOIL Any fertile, moist, well-drained soil

HARDINESS Frost hardy at temperatures down to -5°C/23°F; may need winter protection; leaves are reliably evergreen down to 2°C/38°F

DROUGHT TOLERANCE Poor

PROBLEMS Slugs and snails

CARE Keep moist and do not allow soil to dry out; dry mulch the crown in winter to protect from frosts, or grow in pots and move indoors in winter

PROPAGATION Division in spring

Gaultheria mucronata 'Mulberry Wine' ♗ Wintergreen

⬆ 90cm/3ft ⬌ 1.5m/5ft   EASY

This stylish South American suckering evergreen shrub, with neat, compact growth, has small, oval, deep green leaves (2cm/¾in long) that are spiny-tipped. In late spring it is smothered in tiny, white to pinkish bell-like flowers, which are pretty enough. These are followed by rounded, rich, wine-coloured berries (1.5cm/½in across) that last into winter and are, with the foliage, the plant's best features. This is a female plant, and both male and female plants are needed to ensure berry production; grow a male (such as *G. mucronata*) nearby. *G.m.* 'Bell's Seedling' ♗ has red berries; *G.m.* 'Sneeuwwitje' (syn. *G.m.* Snow White) has white berries.

> **BEST USES** Excellent for low-growing ground cover or as a clipped hedge; ideal in cottage and woodland gardens; good in pots in city gardens

FLOWERS May to June; berries from September

SCENTED No

ASPECT Any, in a sheltered or exposed position; full sun to partial shade

SOIL Any fertile, well-drained soil

HARDINESS Fully hardy at temperatures down to -15°C/5°F; needs no winter protection

DROUGHT TOLERANCE Poor

PROBLEMS None

CARE Trim lightly after flowering, to maintain size and shape

PROPAGATION Detach and pot up rooted suckers in spring; semi-ripe cuttings in summer

Hebe 'Blue Clouds' ♗

⬆ 90cm/3ft ⬌ 90cm/3ft   EASY

Hebes are found from Asia to South America. This rounded, bushy evergreen shrub has narrow, shiny dark green leaves (2cm/¾in long), flushed purple in winter, coupled with rich purple flower spikes (10cm/4in long) that smother the bush from summer to autumn (and often beyond), attracting every bee and butterfly in the vicinity. *H.* 'Champagne' has white flowers; *H.* 'Black Beauty' has moody dark purple foliage and purple flowers.

> **BEST USES** Ideal for coastal, Mediterranean and gravel gardens, hot sunny borders, rock gardens and wildlife gardens; good ground cover for awkward banks and slopes; does well in containers

FLOWERS July to October

SCENTED No

ASPECT Any, in a sheltered position with protection from cold winds; full sun to partial shade

SOIL Any fertile, well-drained soil

HARDINESS Frost hardy at temperatures down to -5°C/23°F; may need winter protection

DROUGHT TOLERANCE Excellent, once established

PROBLEMS Aphids; downy mildew, leaf spot and root rots

CARE Low maintenance; trim lightly in mid-spring if necessary

PROPAGATION Semi-ripe cuttings in a heated propagator in summer; sow ripe seed immediately in pots in a cold frame

Liriope muscari ♂
Lily turf

⬆ 30cm/12in ⬌ 45cm/18in   EASY

This clump-forming tuberous evergreen perennial from China has bright green, grass-like leaves and masses of tiny, baubled, purple-blue flowers (only 6mm/¼in across), packed densely together on sturdy, short, purple pillars; the resulting mauve flower spikes look well against the bladed foliage. It flowers for a long period, from late summer to autumn, when small black berries appear after the flowers. *L.m.* 'Monroe White' has strappy foliage and white flower spikes.

BEST USES Excellent for growing through evergreen ground cover, such as vinca; good for shady corners or woodland; effective ground cover in light shade under shrubs; ideal in pots

FLOWERS August to November
SCENTED No
ASPECT Any, in a sheltered position with protection from cold winds; partial to full shade; can cope with full sun if soil is kept moist
SOIL Any fertile, moist, well-drained soil; add organic matter before planting
HARDINESS Fully hardy at temperatures down to -15°C/5°F; needs no winter protection
DROUGHT TOLERANCE Good, once established
PROBLEMS Slugs and snails like to nibble young foliage
CARE Mulch annually; cut tatty foliage to ground level in spring
PROPAGATION Division in spring

Nandina domestica 'Fire Power' ♂
Heavenly bamboo

⬆ 45cm/18in ⬌ 60cm/24in   EASY

This neat, rounded semi- to fully evergreen shrub from Asia is grown for its warm, fiery red and mellow yellow autumn leaf colour, which persists into winter in mild years. The young spring leaflets are initially flushed pink, maturing by mid-summer to appealing mid-green, filigreed leaves (90cm/3ft long). Small, star-shaped white flowers form pretty enough panicles (40cm/16in long), and are followed by small, rounded green berries that ripen to scarlet. *N.d.* 'Harbour Dwarf' (90cm/3ft) is slightly larger.

BEST USES Excellent ground cover in woodland gardens or covering awkward banks or slopes where mowing is difficult; good as hedging; perfect for smaller cottage gardens and city borders; good for wildlife gardens for berry-foraging birds; often used in bonsai growing

FLOWERS July; grown mainly for autumn foliage
SCENTED No
ASPECT South, west or east facing, in a sheltered or exposed position; full sun to partial shade
SOIL Any fertile, well-drained soil
HARDINESS Frost hardy at temperatures down to -5°C/23°F; may need winter protection
DROUGHT TOLERANCE Good, once established
PROBLEMS None
CARE Remove any dead, diseased or damaged stems, to maintain size and shape
PROPAGATION Semi-ripe cuttings in summer

Ruscus aculeatus
Butcher's broom

⬆ 75cm/30in ⬌ 90cm/3ft   EASY

This Eurasian evergreen is a low-growing, stiffly upright rhizomatous shrublet. It has a bushy habit, densely clothed in small, oval, leathery, polished deep green leaves (2.5cm/1in long), with prickly tips, and never looks scruffy. The tiny, star-shaped, pale green flowers are curious, though not eye-catching, and sit in the centre of the leaves. It is the rounded, vivid scarlet berries, borne in profusion from autumn into winter, that make it a worthwhile foliage plant. Male and female flowers appear on different plants, so you need to grow plants of both sexes to get berries, but this species is often self-fertile, producing its own flowers and fruit.

> **BEST USES** Excellent ground cover in woodland, shady or coastal gardens; good for wildlife gardens, for nesting birds and berry foragers

FLOWERS January to April; berries from September
SCENTED No
ASPECT Any, in a sheltered or exposed position; full sun to full shade
SOIL Any fertile, well-drained soil
HARDINESS Fully hardy at temperatures down to -15°C/5°F; needs no winter protection
DROUGHT TOLERANCE Good, once established
PROBLEMS None
CARE Cut dead stems to ground level in spring
PROPAGATION Division in spring; sow ripe seed immediately in pots in a cold frame

Saxifraga 'Sugar Plum Fairy'
Saxifrage

⬆ 30cm/12in ⬌ 90cm/3ft   EASY

This alpine saxifrage is a creeping, rhizomatous semi-evergreen perennial, found in mountainous areas across Japan. In mild winters, it makes gorgeous pale green carpets from rounded, slightly overlapping, scalloped green-veined leaves (9cm/3½in long). Branching flower stems carry tiny, starry, delicate sugar-pink flowers (8mm/³⁄₈in across) that look pleasingly dainty against the foliage. *S.* 'Black Ruby' has moody brown-black leaves with pink flowers.

> **BEST USES** Excellent camouflage for rock gardens or sharp-draining slopes and banks; ideal at the front of borders; good in pots or containers; useful for woodland and shady garden corners if the soil is reliably free-draining

FLOWERS October to November
SCENTED No
ASPECT South, west or east facing, in a sheltered or exposed position; partial shade
SOIL Any fertile, moist, well-drained soil
HARDINESS Fully hardy at temperatures down to -15°C/5°F; needs no winter protection
DROUGHT TOLERANCE Poor
PROBLEMS Aphids, slugs, snails and vine weevil
CARE Remove spent flower stems
PROPAGATION Division in spring

Elaeagnus pungens 'Frederici'

🡑 2m/6ft 🡘 2m/6ft   **EASY**

This bushy, slow-growing, spreading evergreen shrub from Japan is one of the many beautiful Asian evergreens. It has narrow, wavy-edged, variegated deep green leaves (4cm/1½in long), splashed with buttery-cream marbling, which are appealing enough to grow it for foliage alone. In autumn, its tiny white flowers (only 1cm/⅜in long) form short clusters, and exude the sweetest perfume that is heavenly caught on a crisp autumn day. *E.p.* 'Maculata' has dark yellow/green-edged leaves; *E.p.* 'Goldrim' 🏆 has dark green leaves and golden margins.

> **BEST USES** Ideal for hedging and screening; perfect for clothing awkward slopes when you don't want to mow; an elegant addition to large borders, providing year-round interest

FLOWERS October to November
SCENTED Scented flowers
ASPECT Any, in a sheltered or exposed position; full sun to partial shade
SOIL Any fertile, moist, well-drained soil
HARDINESS Fully hardy at temperatures down to -15°C/5°F; needs no winter protection
DROUGHT TOLERANCE Excellent, once established
PROBLEMS Coral spot
CARE Remove dead, diseased or damaged material in early spring
PROPAGATION Semi-ripe cuttings in summer

Euonymus myrianthus
Evergreen spindletree

🡑 3m/10ft 🡘 4m/13ft   **MEDIUM**

This doesn't look like a spindle at first glance, but it is a delightful, upright, rounded frost-hardy evergreen shrub or tree from western China that should be more widely grown. It has grey-brown bark and is clothed in tapering oval leathery matt leaves. Tiny, star-shaped, greeny yellow flower clusters form at the tips of the stems in late spring, but these are outdone by the autumn berries and leaf colour: small, round, fluted orange berries hang like tiny dried oranges against leaves that transform to red and yellow hues.

> **BEST USES** Unusual plant for hedging and screening; useful as a focal point in a mixed bed or lawn for summer, autumn and winter interest; excellent as a wall shrub

FLOWERS April to May; berries in October
SCENTED No
ASPECT Any, in a sheltered or exposed position; full sun to partial shade
SOIL Any fertile, well-drained soil
HARDINESS Frost hardy at temperatures down to -5°C/23°F; may need winter protection
DROUGHT TOLERANCE Excellent, once established
PROBLEMS None
CARE Low maintenance; occasionally trim after flowering, but only when necessary to maintain shape
PROPAGATION Semi-ripe cuttings in summer

Fatsia japonica ♦

⬆ 2–4m/6–13ft ⬌ 2–4m/6–13ft   EASY

This Japanese evergreen shrub has exotic-looking foliage and is tolerant of both pollution and shade, so is widely planted in city courtyards. It makes a handsome, spreading, rounded shrub, clothed in very obviously lobed, highly polished rich green leaves (40cm/16in across), which are striking in their own right. In autumn, smooth, ghostly white stems hold small, marble-sized, pale green creamy white-capped flowers, which combine to form sculptural spheres (4cm/1½in across), and are followed by small, round, black berries.

BEST USES Ideal for shady city gardens; invaluable for adding exotic foliage to a tropical-style or woodland garden; good for awkward banks and slopes; does well in containers

FLOWERS September to October
SCENTED No
ASPECT South, west or east facing, in a sheltered position with protection from cold winds; full sun to partial shade
SOIL Any fertile, moist, well-drained soil
HARDINESS Frost hardy at temperatures down to -5°C/23°F; may need winter protection
DROUGHT TOLERANCE Excellent, once established
PROBLEMS If placed in a windy spot, cold winds can blacken the leaves
CARE Minimal pruning; remove dead, diseased or damaged material in late spring
PROPAGATION Semi-ripe cuttings in a heated propagator at any time

Olearia paniculata
Daisy bush

⬆ 4m/13ft ⬌ 3m/10ft   EASY

This large and appealing rounded evergreen shrub is commonly used for hedging in its native New Zealand. It has appealing, almost pale olive green leaves (10cm/4in long), with attractive wavy edges, held on cinnamon-coloured stems, with the bonus of tiny, slightly musky, honey-scented, tubular, white daisy-like flowers (1cm/³⁄₈in across) that form generous, branching, fragrant flower domes (15cm/6in tall). O. × *haastii* (2m/6ft) is a more compact choice. All are coastal tolerant.

BEST USES Good as hedging or windbreaks for seaside gardens; ideal for Mediterranean and gravel gardens; good for cottage and wildlife gardens, as the flowers are a honey trap for bees

FLOWERS September to October
SCENTED Scented flowers
ASPECT South or west facing, in a sheltered position with protection from cold winds; full sun
SOIL Any fertile, well-drained soil
HARDINESS Fully hardy/borderline at temperatures down to -15°C/5°F; may need winter protection in cold areas
DROUGHT TOLERANCE Excellent, once established
PROBLEMS None
CARE Trim lightly after flowering
PROPAGATION Semi-ripe cuttings in summer

Pleioblastus viridistriatus 🎖

⬆ 1.5m/5ft ↔ 1.5m/5ft   **EASY**

If you are looking for an architectural, tidy, compact dwarf bamboo, this is amongst the best. It's an upright, slow-growing, non-flowering, multi-stemmed, evergreen Japanese bamboo, with attractive green canes that flush purple with maturity. It has long, narrow, ornamental leaves (18cm/7in long) that are golden yellow, with distinct vertical green striping. Plant in full sun to achieve the best colour.

BEST USES Ideal as a focal point in contemporary gardens; good for low screening or hedging; excellent in troughs and containers

FLOWERS Non-flowering; grown for foliage

SCENTED No

ASPECT South or west facing, in a sheltered position with protection from winds; full sun

SOIL Any fertile, moist, well-drained soil

HARDINESS Fully hardy at temperatures down to -15°C/5°F; needs no winter protection

DROUGHT TOLERANCE Good, once established

PROBLEMS None

CARE Mulch the base of the plant with organic matter in early spring

PROPAGATION Division of rhizomes in spring

GREENFINGER TIP *Even though it is evergreen, cutting this plant hard to ground level in winter will keep it growing low and bushy, with bright foliage*

Pyracantha 'Golden Charmer' 🎖
Firethorn

⬆ 3m/10ft ↔ 3m/10ft   **EASY**

Originating in south-east Europe and Asia, this compact, upright, thorny evergreen shrub spreads as it matures, so can be grown as a free-standing or wall shrub. It has dense, oval, glossy deep green leaves (5cm/2in long) and clusters of small, sweetly scented white flowers in late spring (vicious thorns lurk behind the flowers, so handle carefully when pruning). Generous bunches of small, rounded, golden berries follow the flowers in autumn and are a highlight of the plant. *P.* 'Orange Glow' 🎖 (2.5m/8ft) has orange berries on purple stems.

BEST USES Excellent for hedging or screening, and as a wall shrub; perfect for wildlife gardens; good for woodland or cottage gardens

FLOWERS June; grown mainly for foliage and autumn berries

SCENTED Scented flowers

ASPECT South, west or east facing, in a sheltered or exposed position; full sun to partial shade

SOIL Any fertile, well-drained soil

HARDINESS Fully hardy at temperatures down to -15°C/5°F; needs no winter protection

DROUGHT TOLERANCE Excellent, once established

PROBLEMS Aphids, brown scale and caterpillars; fireblight and pyracantha scab

CARE Prune in winter to maintain size and shape

PROPAGATION Semi-ripe cuttings in a heated propagator in summer

Cotoneaster x *watereri* 'John Waterer' 🎖

⬆ 5m/16ft ⬌ 5m/16ft   **EASY**

Cotoneasters are found from Europe to Asia and are largely grown for their vivid autumn berry display. This fast-growing, semi-evergreen, arching shrub eventually makes a rounded shrub, clothed in small, oval, dark green leaves (10cm/4in long), which are attractively tinted burgundy as autumn sets in. The small, simple, five-petalled white flowers (1cm/³⁄₈in across), with pale yellow centres and black-topped stamens in upward-facing clusters, are followed by heavy bunches of prolific, rounded red berries (6mm/¼in), which smother the plant in autumn.

BEST USES Ideal in a mixed, formal or cottage garden border; good for the wildlife garden; can be grown as a large wall shrub or low hedging

FLOWERS June; berries in September
SCENTED No
ASPECT Any, in a sheltered or exposed position; full sun to partial shade
SOIL Any fertile, well-drained soil
HARDINESS Fully hardy at temperatures down to -15°C/5°F; needs no winter protection
DROUGHT TOLERANCE Excellent, once established
PROBLEMS Aphids and scale insect; fireblight
CARE Trim any unwanted stems after flowering
PROPAGATION Semi-ripe cuttings in late summer

....

GREENFINGER TIP *If you have inherited a large, unruly specimen, prune it hard in spring*

Eriobotrya japonica 🎖
Loquat

⬆ 8m/26ft ⬌ 8m/26ft   **MEDIUM**

This is an unusual, architectural, upright frost-hardy evergreen shrub or tree from Japan and China. It produces spreading branches, clothed in large, smart, oval, pointed-tipped, deeply veined deep green leaves (30cm/12in long), with furry undersides. Tanned clusters of flower buds open to small, hawthorn-scented white flowers in autumn. The flowers can be damaged by winter frosts, so the pale orange pear-shaped fruits are not always reliably produced, but they are more likely after long hot summers and mild winters. This needs a sheltered sunny spot to prosper, but is a handsome plant, offering year-round interest.

BEST USES Ideal for sunny city patios; exotic planted against warm walls; excellent in large pots

FLOWERS September to December
SCENTED Scented flowers
ASPECT South, west or east facing, in a sheltered position; full sun
SOIL Any fertile, well-drained soil, including acid and chalky soils
HARDINESS Frost hardy at temperatures down to -5°C/23°F; may need winter protection
DROUGHT TOLERANCE Poor
PROBLEMS Frost can prevent fruiting
CARE Remove dead, diseased or damaged wood in late winter to early spring
PROPAGATION Semi-ripe cuttings in summer

Eryngium pandanifolium 🎖
Sea holly

⬆ 5m/16ft ⬌ 2m/6ft　　　　　　　　EASY

The architectural sea hollies are taprooted, clump-forming perennials, grown for their spiny metallic leaves and sculptural stems, capped with stiff, spiky flower heads of the most vivid blues or white. Most are herbaceous, but this South American giant is evergreen, with silvery grey-green, sinewy, sword-like leaves (up to 2m/6ft long), with serrated edges. Stiff, branching, self-supporting stems erupt into rounded purple flower heads (each about 1cm/³/₈in long), collared by short bracts, borne well into autumn.

BEST USES Excellent for coastal, gravel and Mediterranean gardens; ideal for wildflower gardens; popular as a dried flower

FLOWERS September to October
SCENTED No
ASPECT South, west or east facing, in a sheltered or exposed position; full sun
SOIL Any moderately fertile to poor, well-drained soil
HARDINESS Fully hardy at temperatures down to -15°C/5°F; needs no winter protection
DROUGHT TOLERANCE Excellent, once established
PROBLEMS Slugs and snails; powdery mildew
CARE Remove spent flower heads or leave as a skeletal feature through winter
PROPAGATION Sow ripe seed immediately in pots in a cold frame; root cuttings in winter

GREENFINGER TIP *Good drainage and a blast of sun are essential for good growth and optimum colour*

Euonymus fortunei 'Silver Queen'
Spindle 'Silver Queen'

⬆ 6m/20ft ⬌ 1.5m/5ft　　　　　　　EASY

An energetic, bushy evergreen shrub of Asian origin, this is densely clothed in oval, glossy dark green leaves (5cm/2in long), with creamy white margins. Tiny pale green flowers, held in small pinhead clusters, are produced in summer and are pretty enough; pale pink berries appear in autumn. It can be used as a low-growing shrub or a tall climber and, by clipping any straying upward stems, it also adapts as low-level ground cover. Spindles work hard all year round and tolerate a wide variety of soils and situations.

BEST USES Excellent ground cover on banks and in shady corners; ideal as climbers or wall shrubs in courtyards, around doors or up low walls

FLOWERS May to June; grown mainly for foliage and autumn berries
SCENTED No
ASPECT Any, in a sheltered or exposed position; full sun to partial shade (leaf variegation is stronger in full sun)
SOIL Any fertile, well-drained soil
HARDINESS Fully hardy at temperatures down to -15°C/5°F; needs no winter protection
DROUGHT TOLERANCE Excellent, once established
PROBLEMS None
CARE Trim in early spring before new growth appears, and remove any plain green foliage
PROPAGATION Softwood or semi-ripe cuttings in summer; sow ripe seed immediately in pots in a cold frame; hardwood cuttings in autumn to late winter

Ilex aquifolium 'Argentea Marginata' ♀
Silver-edged holly

⬆ 15m/50ft ↔ 15m/50ft   **EASY**

This British native is a large female evergreen shrub or tree that is very slow-growing, so can be used as a shrub in the garden. Left to grow naturally, it makes an upright, columnar shape, but nip out the growing tip and it will grow in more rounded fashion. It has typical prickly dark green leaves (7cm/2¾in long) with handsome cream edging, flushed pink when young, and small, dull, flowers in spring (8mm/³⁄₈in). Pea-sized vivid red berries are produced in handsome clusters in autumn. *I.a.* 'Amber' ♀ (6m/20ft) has bright golden berries.

BEST USES Excellent focal point in a formal garden and for topiary; ideal for wildlife gardens; good for hedging, given time and patience

FLOWERS May; grown mainly for foliage and berries in November

SCENTED No

ASPECT Any, in a sheltered or exposed position; full sun

SOIL Any fertile, moist, well-drained soil

HARDINESS Fully hardy at temperatures down to -15°C/5°F; needs no winter protection

DROUGHT TOLERANCE Good, once established

PROBLEMS Aphids and scale insect; *Phytophthora* root rot

CARE Remove dead, diseased or damaged material in late winter/early spring; trim hedges in spring; trim topiary lightly in summer

PROPAGATION Semi-ripe cuttings in late summer to early autumn

Pileostegia viburnoides ♀

⬆ 8m/26ft ↔ 4m/13ft   **EASY**

This exceptional self-clinging evergreen climber from Asia is slow-growing, so it won't outgrow its space too quickly. Long, leathery, glossy green leaves (15cm/6in long) are an appealing feature. Clusters of rounded, baubled flower buds are held on branching stems that blanch attractively white in the summer months; in autumn, the buds open to reveal a hazy froth of milky-white flower panicles (15cm/6in across), resembling lace-cap hydrangeas in shape.

BEST USES Excellent against sheltered walls or fences, including north-facing walls; ideal growing through trees and shrubs

FLOWERS August to October

SCENTED No

ASPECT Any, in a sheltered or exposed position; full sun to full shade (flowering is reduced in shade)

SOIL Any fertile, moist, well-drained soil

HARDINESS Frost hardy at temperatures down to -5°C/23°F; may need winter protection

DROUGHT TOLERANCE Poor

PROBLEMS None, though slow to establish

CARE Remove dead, diseased or damaged material in late winter/early spring; prune to fit in spring; trim hedges in spring; trim topiary lightly in summer

PROPAGATION Layering in spring; semi-ripe cuttings in summer

WINTER

The character of a winter garden is restrained and thoughtful. Now the days are short and the darkening skies descend at far too early an hour. Evergreen trees and shrubs, tipped with frost, stand like steadfast sentinels, with their generous offerings of berries and shelter for our garden birds and wildlife. Prickly-edged hollies adorned in festive berry hangings and cotoneasters aglow with orange baubles remind us of the year past, our successes and disappointments. It is as if nature is allowing us time for reflection. Ponder on ways you can improve your garden next year, perhaps by including some evergreen stalwarts that provide profound winter interest. Use these plants as meditative points within the garden. By mirroring nature's own cycle, we can use this mellow time to embrace renewed belief and positive change.

Bergenia 'Autumn Magic'
Elephant's ears

⬆ 30cm/12in ⬌ 40cm/16in   **EASY**

This clump-forming, rhizomatous evergreen perennial from Asia has large, rounded, leathery, deep green cabbagey leaves (25cm/10in long), flushed purple in autumn and winter and attractively vein-etched, that make classy, understated ground cover. Short, stout, smooth pink stems hold chubby pillars of pink tubular flowers (each flower up to 2.5cm/1in across) in spring, intermittently through summer, and again in autumn. Bergenias love moist, shady locations. *B.* 'Overture' has stunning wine-coloured autumn foliage; *B.* 'Silberlicht' ♈ has nodding white flowers, flushed pale pink.

BEST USES Excellent ground cover in gloomy corners and in woodland or seaside gardens; great for clothing awkward banks and slopes

FLOWERS August to December/repeating April; grown mainly for foliage
SCENTED No
ASPECT Any, in a sheltered or exposed position; full sun to full shade
SOIL Any fertile, moist, well-drained soil
HARDINESS Fully hardy at temperatures down to -15°C/5°F; needs no winter protection
DROUGHT TOLERANCE Good, once established
PROBLEMS Caterpillars, slugs, snails and vine weevil; leaf spot
CARE Remove dead, diseased or damaged material in early spring
PROPAGATION Division of rhizomes in autumn

WINTER SMALL (UP TO 90CM/3FT)

Coronilla valentina subsp. *glauca* 'Citrina' ♀

⬆ 80cm/32in ↔ 80cm/32in   **EASY**

This compact, rounded Mediterranean evergreen shrub, with its small, oval, grey-green leaves (5cm/2in long) looks as though it has no tolerance for cold, but appearances are deceptive; the dainty flowers can brave all but the coldest winters. It has small, scented pea-like pale lemon flowers (1cm/³⁄₈in long) that smell faintly of daffodils and stud the bush prolifically in winter, with slim grey pea pods following the flowers. It has a short respite and off it goes again in spring, flowering intermittently throughout the year.

> **BEST USES** Perfect for sustaining winter interest in the gravel or Mediterranean garden; excellent for a warm sunny border; good in containers

FLOWERS November to March
SCENTED Scented flowers
ASPECT South or west facing, in a sheltered position with protection from cold east winds; full sun
SOIL Any fertile, well-drained soil
HARDINESS Frost hardy at temperatures down to -5°C/23°F; may need winter protection
DROUGHT TOLERANCE Excellent, once established
PROBLEMS None
CARE Cut out damaged or dead wood in early spring or autumn, when the plant is dormant
PROPAGATION Sow ripe seed immediately in pots in a cold frame; semi-ripe cuttings in late summer

Erica carnea 'Myretoun Ruby' ♀
Winter heath

⬆ 15cm/6in ↔ 45cm/18in   **EASY**

You will instantly recognise this dependable, low-lying evergreen shrub from Europe, with its typical small, narrow, dark green leaves. From mid-winter to spring, tiny, scented, dangling, bell-shaped magenta flowers (8mm/³⁄₈in long), with sooty black tips, pack the short, slender stems like a troupe of diminutive ballet dancers. This makes exceptional ground cover on acid soils. *E.c.* 'Adrienne Duncan' ♀ has pinky purple flowers and bronzed foliage; *E.c.* 'Ann Sparkes' ♀ has soft rose flowers and golden foliage.

> **BEST USES** Excellent for both cottage and coastal gardens; reliable ground cover, especially for awkward slopes and banks; good in pots

FLOWERS January to May
SCENTED Scented flowers
ASPECT Any, in a sheltered or exposed position; full sun
SOIL Any fertile, moist, well-drained acid soil
HARDINESS Fully hardy at temperatures down to -15°C/5°F; needs no winter protection
DROUGHT TOLERANCE Good, once established
PROBLEMS None
CARE Trim lightly after flowering, to encourage bushy growth
PROPAGATION Semi-ripe cuttings in mid to late summer

GREENFINGER TIP *Acid soil is recommended, but this will grow in a neutral, well-drained soil; sharp drainage is essential (so no heavy clays)*

Erysimum 'Bowles's Mauve' 🎖
Wallflower

⬆ 75cm/30in ⬌ 60cm/24in **EASY**

This upright, shrubby, evergreen perennial from the eastern Mediterranean is a joy to grow. It has attractive narrow, grey-green leaves (13cm/5in long) which remain a steadfast textured green all year. The pretty, deep mauve flowers, held high on slim, self-supporting olive green stems, are only 1.5cm/½in across, but thousands are produced in the lifetime of one plant. It flowers from late winter until summer's end, and has a tendency to be short-lived, but new plants are easily had.

BEST USES Ideal for wildlife gardens as bees love it; equally at home in the Mediterranean or cottage garden; good for coastal conditions

FLOWERS February to July
SCENTED No
ASPECT South, west or east facing, in a sheltered or exposed position; full sun
SOIL Any fertile, well-drained soil; can be short-lived in heavy clay
HARDINESS Fully hardy at temperatures down to -15°C/5°F; needs no winter protection
DROUGHT TOLERANCE Good, once established
PROBLEMS Flea beetles, slugs and snails; clubroot, downy mildew and white blister
CARE Trim lightly after flowering, to prevent legginess
PROPAGATION Sow seed in pots in a cold frame in spring; heeled softwood cuttings in summer

Helleborous x *hybridus* Harvington double pink **Hellebore/Lenten rose**

⬆ 60cm/24in ⬌ 90cm/3ft **EASY**

Hellebores are clump-forming perennials, offering great evergreen foliage and sculptural, long-lived flowers in tempting colours. This hybrid variety has appealing, deeply cut, tough, leathery dark green leaves (40cm/16in long), with nodding, rose pink double flowers (8cm/3in across) that hang in generous numbers from late winter into mid-spring. *H.* x *h.* Harvington pink speckled has maroon freckles on rose-pink petals; *H.* x *h.* Harvington double white has creamy white flowers; *H.* x *h.* Harvington yellow has pale primrose blooms; *H.* x *h.* Harvington red has deep wine red flowers.

BEST USES Excellent ground cover in a shady or woodland garden; ideal in formal borders

FLOWERS February to April
SCENTED No
ASPECT Any, in a sheltered position; partial shade
SOIL Any fertile, well-drained soil
HARDINESS Fully hardy at temperatures down to -15°C/5°F; needs no winter protection
DROUGHT TOLERANCE Good, once established
PROBLEMS Aphids, slugs and snails
CARE Remove any dead or frost-damaged leaves in February
PROPAGATION Division after flowering

GREENFINGER TIP *The flower colour of hybrids raised from seed can be variable, so they are best propagated by division*

Iris unguicularis
Algerian iris

⬆ 30cm/12in ⬌ 15–30cm/6–12in   **EASY**

Most iris are deciduous and flower in summer, but this small, rhizomatous perennial, from dry, rocky areas of Algeria, is evergreen and brings fragrance and vibrant colour to the winter garden. It has narrow, strap-like evergreen leaves (60cm/24in long) and short, smooth, sturdy stems that bear fragrant, beardless purple flowers (8cm/3in across), with vivid yellow-freckled falls. *I.u.* 'Alba' has creamy white flowers with yellow throats.

> **BEST USES** Ideal for coastal, gravel and Mediterranean gardens; rabbit and deer proof; irresistible to bees; excellent cut flower

FLOWERS November to March
SCENTED Scented flowers
ASPECT South or west facing, in a sheltered position with protection from cold winds; full sun
SOIL Any fertile, well-drained soil (good drainage is essential)
HARDINESS Fully hardy at temperatures down to -15°C/5°F; needs no winter protection
DROUGHT TOLERANCE Excellent, once established
PROBLEMS Slugs and snails
CARE Mulch with organic matter in spring; pull off tatty old leaves
PROPAGATION Division from late summer to autumn

GREENFINGER TIP *The flowers are not frost hardy, so cut them in bud and enjoy them indoors*

Juniperus procumbens 'Bonin Isles'

⬆ 30cm/12in ⬌ 2m/6ft   **EASY**

This dwarf, spreading, coniferous evergreen shrub from Asia has aromatic bark and dense, prickly, yellow-green needles (1.5cm/½in long) that thickly cover the elongated stems. It only grows 1.5cm/½in a year in height; given space, it tends to grow laterally, providing a formal, flat, layered effect, making excellent ground cover. If space is limited, it piles up on itself, forming cascading, tiered layers. It produces small dull, black berries through the year, but these rarely appear on cultivated plants. It is invaluable in providing architectural bones to the garden.

> **BEST USES** Excellent ground cover on banks; ideal in formal and Japanese gardens; good in pots; does well in coastal gardens; deer proof

FLOWERS Non-flowering; grown for foliage
SCENTED Aromatic bark
ASPECT Any, in a sheltered or exposed position; full sun to partial shade
SOIL Any fertile, well-drained soil (good drainage is essential)
HARDINESS Fully hardy at temperatures down to -15°C/5°F; needs no winter protection
DROUGHT TOLERANCE Excellent, once established
PROBLEMS Aphids, caterpillars and scale insects; honey fungus
CARE Remove any damaged material in spring or autumn
PROPAGATION Hardwood cuttings in a heated propagator in autumn

Luzula sylvatica 'Aurea'
Golden woodrush

⬆ 80cm/32in ⬌ 45cm/18in   **EASY**

This grassy, clump-forming, evergreen perennial from southern Europe adds vertical accents to any garden border, and is especially valuable for its bold winter colour. The long, linear, arching green-gold leaves (30cm/12in long) colour to bright yellow in winter, adding a splash of sunlit hummocks on gloomy wintry days. Rather average wispy chestnut brown flower panicles are produced in mid-spring to early summer, but the foliage is the main draw. *L.s.* 'Marginata' has deep green leaves with cream edging.

> **BEST USES** Excellent for prairie planting, gravel and wildflower gardens and cottage borders; useful ground cover in woodland gardens; ideal in bog gardens; good in pots in city gardens or roof terraces

FLOWERS April to June; grown mainly for foliage
SCENTED No
ASPECT Any, in a sheltered or exposed position; full sun to partial shade (leaf colour is best in full sun)
SOIL Any fertile, moist soil
HARDINESS Fully hardy at temperatures down to -15°C/5°F; needs no winter protection
DROUGHT TOLERANCE Poor
PROBLEMS Powdery mildew
CARE Cut back any tatty foliage in spring
PROPAGATION Sow seed in pots in a cold frame in spring or autumn; division in late spring to early summer (at the same time as flowers appear)

Podocarpus nivalis 'Kilworth Cream'

⬆ 90cm/3ft ⬌ 60cm/24in   **EASY**

This dwarf, compact, rounded, coniferous evergreen shrub from mountainous areas in New Zealand has fairly stiff stems, clothed in small, linear, leathery green leaves (2cm/¾in long) which take on a shimmering milky hue in winter. Male plants carry winter clusters of yellow catkins and, after a warm summer, females display upright green cones, flushed pink (3cm/1¼in long). When plants of both sexes are grown, small, rounded red berries are produced (albeit unreliably) in autumn. Fresh young spring growth is an attractive salmon pink. A godsend for the small garden or patio, it is very slow-growing.

> **BEST USES** Excellent ground cover in shady corners and Japanese or woodland gardens; ideal for low hedging; good for clothing awkward banks and slopes; ideal in pots

FLOWERS Non-flowering; grown for foliage
SCENTED No
ASPECT Any, in a sheltered position; partial to full shade
SOIL Any fertile, moist, well-drained soil
HARDINESS Fully hardy at temperatures down to -15°C/5°F; needs no winter protection
DROUGHT TOLERANCE Poor
PROBLEMS None
CARE Remove dead, diseased or damaged material as needed
PROPAGATION Semi-ripe cuttings from any upright shoots in late summer

Sarcococca ruscifolia var. *chinensis* ♀
Christmas box/Sweet box

⬆ 90cm/3ft ⬌ 90cm/3ft   EASY

Christmas box are small evergreen shrubs from Asia, and this dwarf variety is less vigorous than some of the other species, so ideal for smaller spaces. A bushy shrub, with elegant, gently arching stem tips, it has narrow, glossy deep green leaves (6cm/2½in long) and I can guarantee that it never has a bad leaf day, looking good 365 days a year. The incredibly fragrant winter flowers are a bonus: spidery clusters of scented, tubular, creamy flowers (6mm/¼in across) decorate the stems in fair profusion and are followed by rounded red berries. 10/10.

BEST USES Ideal ground cover in shady, woodland, cottage and formal gardens; excellent in small city courtyards; good in pots

FLOWERS December to March

SCENTED Scented flowers

ASPECT Any, in a sheltered position with protection from strong winds; partial to full shade

SOIL Any fertile, well-drained soil

HARDINESS Fully hardy at temperatures down to -15°C/5°F; needs no winter protection

DROUGHT TOLERANCE Good, once established

PROBLEMS None

CARE Minimal; trim lightly after flowering to maintain shape

PROPAGATION Semi-ripe cuttings in summer

Viola cornuta 'Icy But Spicy'
Horned violet

⬆ 20cm/8in ⬌ 40cm/16in   EASY

This rhizomatous creeping evergreen perennial from Spain has slightly notched, oval, mid-green leaves (5cm/2in long) and short, smooth, wiry pale green stems, topped in mild winters with very dainty lobed flowers (1.5cm/½in long) of the loveliest slate blue, with bright yellow eyes, surrounded by deep mauve markings, from late winter through to autumn. Violets rarely disappoint, being well-behaved and low maintenance. *V.c.* 'Yellow King' has pale golden flowers with pale blue freckles; ever-reliable *V.c.* Alba Group ♀ has snow white flowers.

BEST USES Any pot, border or garden (cottage, wildflower, formal, informal, coastal or woodland, Mediterranean or gravel) is enhanced by violets

FLOWERS February to November

SCENTED Scented flowers

ASPECT South, west or east facing, in a sheltered or exposed position; full sun to partial shade

SOIL Any fertile, humus-rich, moist, well-drained soil

HARDINESS Fully hardy at temperatures down to -15°C/5°F; needs no winter protection

DROUGHT TOLERANCE Poor

PROBLEMS Aphids, slugs and snails; powdery mildew

CARE Cut back spent flowers to encourage further flowering; pull up plants as necessary, to restrict spread in unwanted areas

PROPAGATION Division in spring or autumn

Buddleja asiatica
Butterfly bush

⬆ 3m/10ft ⬌ 3m/10ft   EASY

This Asian evergreen species of buddleja is more unusual than the commonly grown *davidii* species. It is a fast-growing, tough, open-topped evergreen shrub, with the trademark long, narrow, deep grey-green leaves (30cm/12in long) with white felt undersides. It comes into flower early, with tiny, freesia-scented flowers forming drooping, white spires (25cm/10in long) like melting icicles, hanging from the bowing stems, making a fragrant focal point in the winter garden. Bliss. It's easy to grow, but slightly less hardy than other species, so is best grown against a sunny wall, fence or hedge.

> **BEST USES** Ideal in the Mediterranean, gravel or cottage garden; good in large pots and containers

FLOWERS November to April
SCENTED Scented flowers
ASPECT South or west facing, in a sheltered position; full sun
SOIL Any fertile, well-drained soil
HARDINESS Frost hardy at temperatures down to -5°C/23°F; may need winter protection
DROUGHT TOLERANCE Excellent, once established
PROBLEMS Caterpillars
CARE Low maintenance; remove spent flowers where practical; tidy up tatty leaves in summer; cut back in winter or early spring to healthy shoots 30cm/12in above ground level (don't cut into old wood)
PROPAGATION Semi-ripe cuttings in summer

Camellia japonica 'Lady Loch'

⬆ 3m/10ft ⬌ 2m/6ft   EASY

Camellias are evergreen shrubs indigenous to Asia, prized for their foliage and opulent, early-flowering blooms in a bewildering array of colours. *C.j.* 'Lady Loch' makes a large, upright shrub, densely clothed in oval, polished, leathery dark green leaves (8cm/3in long). The large, peony-like, cupped, pale salmon pink flowers (5cm/2in across) have white edging like faded silk. *C.j.* 'Lovelight' has loose, rose-like, double white blooms; *C.j.* 'Kramer's Supreme' has deep rich rose-red flowers.

> **BEST USES** Excellent evergreen structure; good focal point in winter and spring borders; ideal in woodland and on banks; can be grown in pots

FLOWERS February to March
SCENTED No
ASPECT South, west or north facing, in a sheltered position; partial to full shade
SOIL Any fertile, well-drained acid soil
HARDINESS Fully hardy at temperatures down to -15°C/5°F; needs no winter protection
DROUGHT TOLERANCE Poor
PROBLEMS Aphids, scale insect and vine weevil; sooty mould, honey fungus and leaf spot
CARE Mulch young hedging with organic matter in spring; clip hedges and topiary in summer
PROPAGATION Semi-ripe cuttings in summer

GREENFINGER TIP *Never plant camellias on an east-facing wall as early sun scorches the flowers*

Daphne bholua 'Jacqueline Postill' ♛

⬆ 4m/13ft ↔ 1.5m/5ft   **EASY**

This upright, sometimes spreading, evergreen shrub from the Himalayas has tough, leathery, lance-shaped, polished, deep green leaves (10cm/4in long). In winter, clusters of tightly furled pink flower buds open to sweetly intoxicating, highly fragranced, simple, shallow, four-petalled flowers of deep rose pink (2cm/¾in wide). Small, rounded black berries entice birds in early summer. It's not quite hardy, but should be fine in mild areas without needing too much fussing. Daphnes are notoriously slow-growing, but worth the wait for the fragrance.

> **BEST USES** Ideal for the cottage garden, or in a formal mixed border; does well in pots in city gardens (keep soil reliably moist)

FLOWERS January to February

SCENTED Scented flowers

ASPECT Any, in a sheltered or exposed position; partial shade

SOIL Any fertile, humus-rich, moist, well-drained soil; add leafmould before planting

HARDINESS Fully hardy/borderline at temperatures down to -15°C/5°F; may need winter protection in cold areas

DROUGHT TOLERANCE Poor

PROBLEMS Slugs and snails

CARE Trim lightly after flowering, removing dead, diseased or damaged wood

PROPAGATION Semi-ripe cuttings in mid to late summer

Garrya elliptica
Silk tassel bush

⬆ 4m/13ft ↔ 4m/13ft   **EASY**

From the USA, this is a very restrained and elegant evergreen shrub (or small tree) with a stately, upright habit. It has oval, slightly crimped-edged, deep grey-green leaves (8cm/3in across), that are lightly lustred, with woolly undersides. From winter into early spring, silky tasselled catkins of pale sage green (15–20cm/6–8in long) dangle in tiered splendour from smooth brown-grey stems, like an ornamental chandelier. It is slow-growing, and will take about twenty years to reach its full height. *G.e.* 'James Roof' ♛ has particularly long silvery catkins (20cm/8in).

> **BEST USES** Valuable focal point in a formal border; good trained as a wall shrub in sheltered courtyards or patios; good for coastal gardens

FLOWERS January to March

SCENTED No

ASPECT Any, in a sheltered position with protection from cold winds; full sun to partial shade

SOIL Any fertile, well-drained soil

HARDINESS Frost hardy at temperatures down to -5°C/23°F; may need winter protection

DROUGHT TOLERANCE Good, once established

PROBLEMS Leaf spot

CARE Remove dead, diseased or damaged material in late spring

PROPAGATION Semi-ripe cuttings in summer; sow seed in pots in a cold frame in autumn

Grevillea rosmarinifolia ♀

⬆ 3m/10ft ⬌ 1–5m/3–16ft   EASY

This bushy, spreading, evergreen shrub is used as ornamental hedging in its native Australia. It has upward, branching stems, thickly clothed with stiff, bright to grey-green needle-like leaves (5cm/2in long) that look very similar to rosemary. Clusters of spidery, pinky red flowers (7cm/2¾in long) explode between the needled stem tips like painted talons or decorative lanterns, from autumn well into early summer. Though averse to frost, it is becoming borderline hardy in the UK. *G.r.* 'Jenkinsii' has creamy pink flowers.

BEST USES Good for colour in Mediterranean or tropical gardens; ideal in pots and conservatories; worth trying as hedging in mild areas

FLOWERS November to June
SCENTED No
ASPECT Any, in a sheltered position; full sun to partial shade
SOIL Any fertile, well-drained, slightly acid soil
HARDINESS Frost hardy at temperatures down to -5°C/23°F; may need winter protection
DROUGHT TOLERANCE Excellent, once established
PROBLEMS None
CARE Trim lightly after flowering
PROPAGATION Semi-ripe cuttings in summer

GREENFINGER TIP *Although described as an acid-loving plant, I have grown this successfully in sandy soil (I doubt it will cope with heavy clay)*

Hardenbergia violacea ♀
False sarsparilla

⬆ 2.5m/8ft ⬌ 2m/6ft   EASY

An energetic, twining, woody evergreen climber from Australia, this has long, pointed, leathery grey-green leaves (12cm/4½in long) and tiny pea-like violet flowers (1cm/³⁄₈in long) (with the odd pink or white renegade among them). The flowers form dense, pendulous clusters (13cm/5in long), dangling enticingly in winter. This is not fully hardy, but should survive easily in frost-free areas or when grown on a warm, sheltered wall.

BEST USES Good in a container in a sunny, city garden or on a lightly dappled patio; ideal trained against trellis or up small arbours and pergolas

FLOWERS January to March
SCENTED No
ASPECT South or west facing, in a sheltered position; full sun to partial shade
SOIL Any fertile, well-drained soil; add organic matter before planting
HARDINESS Frost hardy at temperatures down to -5°C/23°F; may need winter protection
DROUGHT TOLERANCE Good, once established
PROBLEMS None outdoors; aphids and red spider mite when grown indoors
CARE Prune lightly after flowering to maintain size and shape; protect with fleece or move indoors in winter; if growing in a conservatory, feed once a month with liquid feed
PROPAGATION Sow pre-soaked seed in a heated greenhouse or propagator at 20°C/68°F in spring; softwood cuttings in spring

Ilex aquifolium 'Golden van Tol'

⬆ 4m/13ft ↔ 3m/10ft   **EASY**

This large, slow-growing, female, hardy evergreen shrub or small tree makes an upright, columnar shape when left to grow naturally, but will grow in a more rounded fashion (and stay smaller) when the growing tip is nipped out. Smooth, vivid deep mauve stems are clothed in prickly dark green leaves (7cm/2¾in long), with buttery yellow edging. Small, dull flowers (8mm/⅜in) appear in late spring to early summer and rounded, pea-sized red berries are produced in late autumn, though not in great numbers.

> **BEST USES** Ideal slow-growing hedging; excellent topiary in a formal garden; good for wildlife gardens as berries are a reliable food source

FLOWERS May to June; grown mainly for foliage
SCENTED No
ASPECT Any, in a sheltered or exposed position; full sun to partial shade
SOIL Any fertile, moist, well-drained soil
HARDINESS Fully hardy at temperatures down to -15°C/5°F; needs no winter protection
DROUGHT TOLERANCE Good, once established
PROBLEMS Aphids, scale insect and leaf miners; *Phytophthora* root rot
CARE Remove dead, diseased or damaged material in late winter/early spring; trim hedges in spring; trim topiary lightly in summer
PROPAGATION Semi-ripe cuttings in late summer to early autumn

Mahonia lomariifolia ♀
Burmese mahonia

⬆ 3m/10ft ↔ 2m/6ft   **MEDIUM**

Mahonias are uncomplicated, reliable evergreens, and this arching shrub from China probably has the best foliage of all the species. The large, glossy, deeply divided, toothed deep green leaves (60cm/24in long) look rather like leathery fern fronds and are arranged in layered, circular fashion around the tough, brawny stems. Tiny, lily of the valley-scented, dark primrose yellow flowers form large, upright candle-like clusters (20cm/8in long) from autumn into winter, followed by rounded black berries. Although not fully hardy, there's not much to match it for year-round elegance, fragrance and architectural interest.

> **BEST USES** Excellent in cottage, formal or woodland gardens; good for shady city borders

FLOWERS November to January
SCENTED Scented flowers
ASPECT North, east or west facing, in a sheltered position; partial to full shade
SOIL Any fertile, well-drained soil
HARDINESS Frost hardy at temperatures down to -5°C/23°F; may need winter protection
DROUGHT TOLERANCE Good, once established
PROBLEMS None
CARE Prune after flowering; can be cut back hard if plant gets leggy with no bottom growth
PROPAGATION Semi-ripe cuttings in late summer to autumn

Sophora Sun King ♟
Japanese pagoda tree

🡑 3m/10ft 🡘 3m/10ft   EASY

This large, spreading, evergreen shrub or small tree from the Far East is one of the hardiest of the species. Pairs of small, oval, rounded dark green leaves (15cm/6in long) make a small, mounding, arching, open shrub. From early spring, generous numbers of small, drooping, dark yellow flowers form pendulous flower clusters (5cm/2in long) that last for some weeks.

BEST USES Excellent as a large shrub in gravel and Mediterranean or coastal gardens; good for sunny city patios or courtyard gardens as a wall shrub; ideal in container gardens

FLOWERS February to March

SCENTED No

ASPECT Any, in a sheltered or exposed position; full sun

SOIL Any fertile, well-drained soil

HARDINESS Fully hardy at temperatures down to -15°C/5°F; needs no winter protection

DROUGHT TOLERANCE Poor

PROBLEMS None

CARE Low maintenance; in late winter to early spring, remove dead, diseased or damaged material or, if growing as a wall shrub, trim to maintain size and shape

PROPAGATION Semi-ripe cuttings in a heated propagator in summer or autumn

Viburnum tinus 'Eve Price' ♟

🡑 3m/10ft 🡘 3m/10ft   EASY

This popular, bushy evergreen Mediterranean shrub is one of the more compact, bushy viburnum cultivars, with elegant, glossy oval leaves (8cm/3in long) and clusters of tiny, sweetly scented star-shaped flowers that form domed flower heads (10cm/4in long) that are blossom pink in bud, opening to white, from winter well into spring. Generous bunches of deep purple-black berries are produced in autumn, often at the same time as the flowers.

BEST USES Good for year-round interest in a formal or cottage garden; ideal for wildlife gardens; good in coastal gardens as a hedge or windbreak

FLOWERS December to April

SCENTED No

ASPECT Any, in a sheltered position with protection from cold winds; full sun to full shade

SOIL Any fertile, well-drained soil

HARDINESS Fully hardy at temperatures down to -15°C/5°F; needs no winter protection

DROUGHT TOLERANCE Excellent, once established

PROBLEMS Aphids (whitefly) and viburnum beetles; *Botrytis* (grey mould), honey fungus and leaf spot

CARE Low maintenance; remove dead or damaged material in late winter or early spring to retain size and shape

PROPAGATION Layering in spring; semi-ripe cuttings in mid-summer to autumn; hardwood cuttings in winter

Buxus sempervirens ♉
Common box

⬆ 5m/16ft ⬌ 5m/16ft   EASY

Box is a bushy, evergreen, large shrub or small tree. Clipped regularly, it will make a tight, dense-leaved, rounded shrub, with tiny, rounded, polished leaves (3cm/1¼in long), and can be trained into almost any shape. Alternatively, grow it as a neat, formal, mounded tree. Tiny, starry, pale yellow flowers sit in the leaf joints in spring. It grows at a reasonable pace if fed from the outset. *B.s.* 'Elegantissima' ♉ has silver white-margined leaves; *B.s* 'Suffruticosa' ♉ (90cm/3ft) is ideal for dwarf hedging.

> **BEST USES** Excellent as evergreen structure and hedging; good in pots as topiary

FLOWERS April to May; grown mainly for foliage
SCENTED No
ASPECT Any, in a sheltered or exposed position; partial to full shade
SOIL Any fertile, well-drained soil
HARDINESS Fully hardy at temperatures down to -15°C/5°F; needs no winter protection
DROUGHT TOLERANCE Excellent, once established
PROBLEMS Red spider mite; box blight and leaf spot
CARE Mulch young hedging with organic matter in spring; clip hedges and topiary in summer
PROPAGATION Semi-ripe cuttings in summer

GREENFINGER TIP *Clip topiary in late spring and again around Derby Day (early June); add blood, fish and bone to the base and water well*

Clematis cirrhosa 'Jingle Bells'

⬆ 5m/16ft ⬌ 2m/6ft   EASY

This lovely upwardly scrambling tendrilled evergreen climber is a winter wonder from the Balearic Islands, so it appreciates a warm sheltered spot. It has dainty, dissected, glossy deep green leaves that bronze slightly in winter and produces charming, nodding, creamy white flowers (8cm/3in across) with a lemony fragrance that sit prettily against the smart foliage. The delicate flowers are followed by attractive silvery seed heads. It has a moderate growth rate, so is ideal for small gardens, and grows happily in pots (position them by a doorway to enjoy the fragrance).

> **BEST USES** Excellent for pergolas, arbours and walkways where you don't want a rampant climber; ideal for growing through deciduous shrubs

FLOWERS December to February
SCENTED Scented flowers
ASPECT South or west facing, in a sheltered position; full sun
SOIL Any fertile, well-drained soil
HARDINESS Frost hardy at temperatures down to -5°C/23°F; may need winter protection
DROUGHT TOLERANCE Poor
PROBLEMS None
CARE Low maintenance; if you need to curb its spread, prune overlong shoots back to healthy buds immediately after flowering (Group 1)
PROPAGATION Internodal semi-ripe cuttings in late summer; layering in late summer to autumn

Clematis napaulensis

⬆ 10m/32ft ⬌ 3m/10ft   **EASY**

This energetic, tendrilled, clasping, woody-based semi-evergreen climber of Asian origin doesn't really look much for most of the year: despite its evergreen pedigree it loses most of its leaves during the summer. However, new elliptical, lance-shaped, fresh green leaves burst forth with surprising vigour in autumn. Come late winter, very attractive, tremulous, pendent clusters of sweetly fragrant, bell-shaped, greeny cream flowers (2cm/¾in long) peel back charmingly to reveal conspicuous purple-red stamens protruding from each intriguing flower. The flowers are succeeded by fluffy seed heads.

BEST USES Good on a wall or fence near the house; excellent for winter interest in cottage or country gardens; good growing through bare shrubs; ideal in pots for city patios

FLOWERS November to March
SCENTED Scented flowers
ASPECT South or west facing, in a sheltered position; full sun to partial shade
SOIL Any fertile, well-drained soil
HARDINESS Fully hardy at temperatures down to -15°C/5°F; needs no winter protection
DROUGHT TOLERANCE Poor
PROBLEMS Clematis wilt
CARE Prune back after flowering, to keep tidy (Group 1)
PROPAGATION Internodal semi-ripe cuttings in mid to late summer; layering in late summer to early autumn

Hedera colchica 'Sulphur Heart' 🏅
(syn. 'Paddy's Pride') Persian ivy

⬆ 5m/16ft ⬌ 5m/16ft   **EASY**

This very vigorous, fast-growing, self-clinging evergreen climber from Iran has large, elongated heart-shaped glossy dark green leaves (13cm/5in long) that curl under at the edges and are splashed with creamy yellow marbling which becomes more vivid as the leaves age. In autumn, it bears fist-sized domes of limey green flower clusters, made up of tiny, individual green flowers, which are irresistible to bees.
H.c. 'Dentata Variegata' 🏅 has marbled, cream grey-green leaves.

BEST USES Excellent ground cover in shady areas or on awkward banks; useful for screening eyesores; good for wildlife gardens

FLOWERS October to November; grown mainly for foliage
SCENTED No
ASPECT Any, in a sheltered position; full sun to full shade
SOIL Any fertile, well-drained soil; add organic matter before planting
HARDINESS Fully hardy at temperatures down to -15°C/5°F; needs no winter protection
DROUGHT TOLERANCE Excellent, once established
PROBLEMS Aphids and scale insect; leaf spot
CARE Low maintenance; mulch annually in early spring; cut back as required to restrict height or spread at any time
PROPAGATION Semi-ripe cuttings in summer

Evergreen trees

Evergreen trees, whether coniferous or broad-leaved, play an important role in our garden structure. We may feature them as elegant specimens in a lawn or use them to provide screening from roads and neighbours and as hedges or divisions within the garden. They always need to be sited with care, as they will be part of the landscape for many years. Think twice, plant once.

When choosing a tree, first consider its shape and foliage. Trees may be mounding, rounded, conical, spreading, ground hugging or weeping, for example. As well as the coniferous trees, which have needled foliage, there are a great many trees that have broad, polished, ornamental leaves, and these offer a perfect backdrop to our garden scenery.

Some conifers, such as pines and cedar, also provide the benefit of lovely woody aromas. (The term 'conifer' applies to any tree that produces cones, which will take between one and three years to ripen fully; they usually start off green, becoming brown as they mature.)

Almost all the trees listed here are easy to grow. Most evergreen trees need little or no pruning, but hedges will need cutting (which is really just a form of pruning) to keep them manageable. Trees and hedges need regular watering for the first three years, but after that they are self-sustaining. A few might prefer special conditions, and information is given about these in their profiles; for example, some will not tolerate cold winds, so it is important to plant them in a sheltered spot.

Different species have different growth rates. In warm climates, some trees can attain their full height in less than thirty years, but others may take a hundred years or more. Many are so slow-growing that they remain small, almost shrub-sized, after ten years. These are suitable for smaller gardens or can even be planted in large containers.

The height and spread in 10–20 years have been given here, but some will eventually exceed these measurements. Be sensible; plant small trees in small spaces. Of course, if you have the luxury of acres, then the world is your lobster.

ABIES Silver fir

This group of architectural, hardy coniferous trees comes from Asia, Europe and North America. Ranging in size from dwarf to some 45m/150ft in height, they will grow in any moist, well-drained, slightly acid soil and tolerate shade as well as sun.

Abies koreana 'Silberlocke'

↑ 4m/13ft ⟷ 1.5m/5ft   EASY

A slow-growing, bushy, pyramid-shaped, hardy evergreen conifer from Korea; the needled foliage is dark green, with silver-blue undersides; the cones are violet blue.

Abies nordmanniana 'Golden Spreader'

↑ 1.5m/5ft ⟷ 90cm/3ft   EASY

A slow-growing, dwarf, hardy evergreen conifer from northern Turkey, with a typical, bushy, Christmas-tree shape and green-yellow needled foliage, flushed bright gold in winter; the cones are light brown.

Arbutus unedo 'Compacta'

↑ 3.5m/12ft ⟷ 3m/10ft   EASY

A large, hardy evergreen shrubby tree from the Mediterranean, with a dense, branching habit and peeling red-brown bark; the leathery oval leaves are dark green and pendent strings of white flowers, flushed pink, appear in autumn, with small, strawberry-like fruits in autumn to winter. Easy to grow in any well-drained soil, in sun or partial shade; drought tolerant, and ideal for coastal areas.

CEDRUS Cedar

The fully hardy coniferous cedars make elegant specimen trees in lawns. They are easy to grow and thrive on any well-drained soil, in a sunny spot.

Cedrus atlantica 'Aurea'

↑ 5m/16ft ⟷ 1.5m/5ft   EASY

A dwarf, slow-growing, conical, hardy evergreen conifer from the Lebanon, with drooping branch tips; mature trees flatten at the top and branches spread horizontally. The young needle-like foliage is bright yellow in spring, maturing to dark green in summer; large grey-pink cones are held upright on the branches, taking two years to ripen over autumn to winter.

Cedrus atlantica Glauca Group 'Glauca Pendula'

⬆ 5m/16ft ⬌ 10m/32ft **EASY**

A hardy evergreen conifer from the Lebanon, with a stiff, arching, weeping habit, clothed in silver-blue needles, and greenish brown oval cones. It grows about 30cm/12in annually; to restrict its size, use a stake or support: once the 'leader' (or central growing tip) reaches the top of the stake, the branches begin to weep downward, and it won't grow any taller than its supported height.

Cedrus deodara 'Golden Horizon'

⬆ 2m/6ft ⬌ 2m/6ft **EASY**

A fairly slow-growing, mound-forming, spreading, architectural, dwarf, hardy evergreen conifer from the Himalayas, with weeping branch tips; the young needle-like foliage is bright yellow in spring, maturing to darker green in summer, and oval, pinky red egg-shaped cones are an appealing feature. Its layered, weeping branches make ideal ground cover.

CEPHALOTAXUS Plum yew

These small, slow-growing, multi-stemmed, fully hardy evergreen coniferous trees or shrubs from Asia are neat, versatile plants, ideal for hedging, woodland gardens or as solitary focal points. Male and female flowers appear on separate plants. They prefer moist, well-drained, fertile soil in partial shade, with protection from winds. They are drought tolerant and deer proof.

Cephalotaxus harringtonia 'Fastigiata'

⬆ 5m/16ft ⬌ 5m/16ft **EASY**

A small, dense, bushy, hardy evergreen conifer from Korea, similar to yew in appearance, with an upright, vase-shaped habit; it has smooth, deep green needled leaves, with bright yellow shoots when young. Female plants produce rounded, fleshy, pea-sized green berries, maturing to red then brown. Good for chalky soil.

Cephalotaxus harringtonia 'Korean Gold'

⬆ 1.5m/5ft ⬌ 90cm/3ft **EASY**

A small, shrubby, columnar, hardy evergreen conifer from Korea, with peeling red-brown bark, long gold-tipped needles (7cm/3in) that mature to deep green in winter, and appealing small plum-like fruits. Ideal for tight spaces.

CHAMAECYPARIS False cypress

This large group of fully hardy coniferous trees, originating from America to Asia, has many varieties, ranging from tall, upright, pyramid shapes to those with small, rounded or layered habits. The medium-sized varieties are ideal as hedging, while the slower-growing dwarf forms will suit Oriental-style or rock gardens. Many have golden foliage, which colours up best when planted in full sun. They will grow in any well-drained soil, including chalk, in a sunny position.

Chamaecyparis pisifera 'Boulevard' 🏅

⬆ 4m/13ft ⬌ 2m/6ft **EASY**

A dense, conical, hardy evergreen conifer from Japan, with soft, tactile, blue-green foliage, often tipped purple in winter, and small rounded cones. Prefers a moist soil.

Chamaecyparis pisifera 'Golden Mop' 🏅

⬆ 90cm/3ft ⬌ 90cm/3ft **EASY**

A rounded, mop-headed, slow-growing, hardy evergreen conifer from Japan, with flattened golden foliage; cones are rarely produced. Suitable for small beds, borders and containers.

Chamaerops humilis 🏅 Dwarf fan palm (above)

⬆ 3m/10ft ⬌ 2m/6ft **MEDIUM**

A half-hardy palm (withstanding temperatures down to 0°C/32°F) from the Mediterranean, with large, tough, deeply divided, fan-like, architectural evergreen leaves. It prefers well-drained, fertile to poor soil, in full sun, with protection from cold winds; can be grown outside in milder areas, with fleece wrapped round it in winter, or brought inside until the summer.

CRYPTOMERIA Japanese cedar

These extremely slow-growing, upright, fully hardy evergreen coniferous trees from Asia have mahogany red bark, with short, deep green needled foliage and rounded female cones or conical male cones at the tips of the branches. They are among the few evergreen trees that will shoot again after hard pruning. Grow in any well-drained soil in full sun to partial shade, with protection from winds. They are ideal for Oriental-style planting, in small gardens or pots, and for use as screening or ground cover.

Cryptomeria japonica 'Globosa Nana'

⬆ 90cm/3ft ⬌ 90cm/3ft   EASY

A slow-growing, neat, elegant, rounded, dwarf, hardy evergreen conifer from Japan, with blue-green needles, tinted rust in winter (the colder it is, the rustier they get) and round, green-brown cones in autumn to winter.

Cryptomeria japonica 'Golden Promise'

⬆ 60cm/24in ⬌ 50cm/20in   EASY

A small, rounded, dwarf, hardy evergreen conifer from Japan, with bright green foliage that turns soft gold in summer, and purple-tinted leaves in winter; green cones mature to brown.

Cryptomeria japonica 'Vilmoriniana'

⬆ 90cm/3ft ⬌ 90cm/3ft   EASY

A rounded, dwarf, hardy evergreen conifer from Japan, with reddish-brown bark, clothed in dense, stubby, deep green needles, tinted burgundy in winter, with small, rounded brown cones.

Cunninghamia lanceolata 'Little Leo'

⬆ 15cm/6in ⬌ 30cm/12in   EASY

A slow-growing, dwarf, hardy evergreen conifer from China (about 5cm/2in growth a year), making a compact, low-growing, bun-shaped tree, with bright green needles, tinted purple in winter, conker brown bark, and small, bud-like brown cones. Grow in fertile, well-drained soil, in full sun to partial shade, with protection from winds.

CUPRESSUS Cypress

Found widely across the northern hemisphere, cypress are among my favourite coniferous trees, with their narrow, conical or columnar architectural habit. They hate clipping and make great screening material; they can also be grown in pots. Lopping the tops off keeps them shorter and columnar. They enjoy well-drained soil in full sun, with shelter from winds, and are drought tolerant.

Cupressus sempervirens 'Green Pencil'

⬆ 15m/50ft ⬌ 2.5m/8ft   EASY

An upright, pencil-shaped, elegant, architectural, hardy evergreen conifer from the Mediterranean, made famous by Vincent van Gogh, with fragrant bark, densely clothed in tough, scaly, flattened, deep grey-green foliage; small, hard, rounded green cones mature to brown over two years. On young trees, the weight of the cones can cause the boughs to sag; to prevent this, remove the cones.

Cupressus sempervirens 'Swane's Gold'

⬆ 6m/20ft ⬌ 90cm/3ft   EASY

A tall, narrow, columnar, architectural, hardy evergreen conifer from the Mediterranean, with tough, scaly, erect gold-yellow foliage, and hard, prickly, green-brown cones.

EUCALYPTUS Gum tree

Eucalyptus are fast-growing Australian natives, grown for their attractive, aromatic foliage and interesting bark, in colours from silver grey to chestnut and copper tones. Most are only suitable for large gardens, unless they are kept small by annual pruning (or coppicing) to 25cm/10in above ground level in spring. This also keeps the foliage young and at its best. The hardier, smaller varieties, which can be coppiced to keep them manageable or grown in pots to restrict their size, are included here. Grow in any well-drained soil in full sun, in a sheltered spot; they are tough and drought tolerant.

Eucalyptus gregsoniana

⬆ 4m/13ft ⬌ 5m/16ft   EASY

A frost-hardy evergreen tree from Australia, with creamy bark and attractive red leaf shoots when young, maturing to small, crescent-shaped grey-blue leaves; yellow buds open to tiny white flowers in spring to summer.

EUCHRYPHIA Leatherwood

This highly ornamental, fragrant-flowered, evergreen and deciduous group of trees from Australasia ranges from fully hardy to frost-hardy species. They are natural woodlanders, so prefer fertile, neutral to acid, moist soil in full sun to partial shade; shade roots by underplanting, and provide shelter from winds. They will grow well given ideal conditions, but otherwise may prove a struggle.

Euchryphia cordifolia x lucida

⬆ 4m/13ft ⬌ 3m/10ft   **MEDIUM**

A slow-growing, frost-hardy, hybrid evergreen tree of South American and Tasmanian origin, with appealing wavy-edged, glossy dark green oblong leaves (up to 6cm/2½in long) and large, white fragrant flowers from late summer to early autumn.

Euchryphia milliganii

⬆ 4m/13ft ⬌ 1.5m/5ft   **MEDIUM**

A lovely frost-hardy evergreen shrubby tree from Tasmania with a slender, upright habit and dense, glossy, deep green leaves; shallow-cupped white flowers (up to 2cm/¾in across) appear from mid to late summer.

JUNIPERUS Juniper

This group of hardy coniferous trees and shrubs hails from across the northern hemisphere and includes plants that will suit most soils and locations, offering architectural shapes and needles of diverse colour, in tall specimens as well as dwarf, low-growing types that make excellent ground cover. Male cones and female berries appear on separate plants. They rarely need pruning and will grow in any well-drained soil, in full sun to partial shade, in both sheltered and exposed conditions.

Juniperus communis 'Repanda' ♔ (right)

⬆ 60cm/24in ⬌ 2.5m/8ft   **EASY**

A ground-hugging, carpeting, hardy evergreen tree or large shrub, found across the northern hemisphere, that grows wider than it is tall; deep green needles are often tipped bronze in winter, and small, bud-like glaucous green berries ripen to black over a three-year period.

LIGUSTRUM Privet

This group of semi- to fully evergreen hardy shrubs or small trees from Asia offers gardeners real alternatives to fast-growing coniferous hedging such as *leylandii* and will prove more manageable. They are attractive in terms of flower and foliage and make superior hedging. (Hedges need only be clipped at least twice from June onwards to keep them bushy and dense.) Nurseries often sell privets as quarter and half-standard topiary or on stilts for instant tall hedging. Privet is easy to grow in any well-drained soil, in full sun to partial shade, though the variegated types have better leaf colour if planted in full sun.

Ligustrum japonicum Japanese privet

⬆ 3m/10ft ⬌ 2.5m/8ft   **EASY**

A dense, upright, fully hardy evergreen shrub from Japan, with polished deep green leaves and musty-smelling white flower sprays (up to 15cm/6in long) from early autumn, followed by black berries.

Ligustrum lucidum 'Excelsum Superbum' ♔ Chinese privet

⬆ 4m/13ft ⬌ 2.5m/8ft   **EASY**

A conical, fully hardy evergreen tree, from China, Korea and Japan, with long, tapering, polished bright green leaves with variegated yellow edges, and plentiful panicles of frothy white flowers from late summer to early autumn, followed by rounded blue-black berries.

Ligustrum ovalifolium 'Aureum'
Golden privet (right)

⬆ 4m/13ft ↔ 4m/13ft   EASY

A fully hardy evergreen to semi-evergreen shrub from Japan, with smart oval, glossy, bright green-centred leaves (up to 6cm/2½in long) with bright yellow edges, and large sprays of white flowers in mid-summer, followed by rounded black berries; one of the superior privets in my view, for its smashing golden hues.

PINUS Pine
This huge group of evergreen coniferous trees comes from across the northern hemisphere to Asia and South America. The trees are bushy, often flat-topped, with bunches of long needled foliage and shapely cones that remain on the trees for some years. They are unfussy about soil as long as it is not waterlogged (although they are short-lived in chalky soil), and thrive in the poorest soils and in coastal areas. Grow in well-drained soil, in full sun.

Pinus mugo 'Mops' Dwarf mountain pine

⬆ 90cm/3ft ↔ 90cm/3ft   EASY

A very slow-growing (about 5cm/2in per year), compact, rounded, bushy, dwarf, hardy evergreen conifer from central Europe, with mid-green needles and small, dark brown cones, ripening over two to three years.

Pinus sylvestris 'Gold Coin'

⬆ 2m/6ft ↔ 2m/6ft   EASY

A small, conical, slow-growing, fully hardy evergreen conifer from North America, with green needles turning a striking golden yellow in winter; small, oval, reddish cones are produced in winter, ripening to brown over two to three years.

Pseudotsuga menziesii 'Fletcheri'
Douglas fir

⬆ 2m/6ft ↔ 2m/6ft   EASY

A very slow-growing, fully hardy evergreen from North America, making a rounded, flat-topped, spreading, tiered tree with corky, conker brown bark when mature and aromatic, loose, blue-green needles and large brown cones in autumn to winter. Grow in any well-drained soil except chalk, in full sun.

SEQUOIA SEMPERVIRENS
Californian redwood
Redwoods are fast-growing evergreen trees from the USA. The famous Giant redwood grows up to 112m/367ft, but there are smaller, hardy varieties that are suitable for smaller spaces. They are ideal for hedging, screening and garden divisions, and are among the few conifers that will sprout again from the base after coppicing. Grow in any well-drained soil, in full sun to partial shade, in a sheltered spot. Good for coastal gardens.

Sequoia sempervirens 'Prostrata'

⬆ 15cm/6in ↔ 1.2m/4ft   EASY

A dwarf, fully hardy evergreen conifer from coastal California with a spreading habit and slightly pendulous branches, densely clothed in flat, grey-green needles, completely masking the red, corky bark; small cones typically ripen to dark brown over two years. Makes excellent ground cover (to keep a low, domed shape, nip out any stems that grow upright).

TAXUS Yew

This group of long-lived coniferous shrubs or small hardy evergreen trees originates from across Europe, Iran and North Africa. Non-flowering, they are grown for their formal, textural and architectural habit. They have red-brown bark with narrow, linear, deep green leaves and soft, juicy, vivid red berries which are poisonous and best left to the birds.

They are very versatile, being effective as winter accent shrubs, hedging and topiary, while the low-growing forms make good ground cover. When grown as hedging, plant individual plants 45cm/18in apart, in single or double rows; they will need pruning once the hedge is established, but are among the rare evergreens that will tolerate very hard pruning and still re-grow. They are easy to grow, in sun to full shade, in any well-drained soil, including chalky and acid soil, and are both pollution and drought tolerant.

Taxus baccata 'Dovastonii Aurea'

⬆ 3m/10ft ⬌ 2m/6ft   EASY

A fully hardy evergreen female tree or large shrub from across Europe, Iran and North Africa, elegantly attired with draping branches, clothed in narrow, golden-edged yellow leaves; trademark red berries appear in autumn. Initially slow-growing, this can grow up to 40cm/16in a year once established.

Taxus baccata Fastigiata Aurea Group

⬆ 3m/10ft ⬌ 90cm/3ft   EASY

This densely clothed, chunky, pillared, fully hardy evergreen tree from Europe has glossy, flattened, deep green needle-like leaves (1cm/⅜in long), edged in gold, held on pliable, upright green-yellow stems that create a stepped effect; toxic, rounded, soft, juicy, pea-sized red berries are produced from late autumn into winter, and exude a clear gel-like substance when squashed.

Taxus baccata 'Standishii'

⬆ 1.5m/5ft ⬌ 60cm/24in   EASY

A small, columnar, fully hardy evergreen tree from Europe, with dense, linear, gold-green leaves on radial branches, forming a very upright, chunky-looking pillar; it has red berries in autumn. Ideal for small gardens, as it needs no pruning or trimming.

THUJA Western red cedar

Hailing from Asia and North America, these fully hardy evergreen coniferous trees are conical in shape, with flat, scaly, aromatic foliage, decorative cones and furrowed grey bark. The flat-topped and mounding forms need little maintenance, but species grown as hedging will need a trim twice a year, in spring and summer. They grow in moist (not waterlogged), well-drained, fertile soil, in full sun, with shelter from cold or drying winds.

Thuja occidentalis 'Danica'

⬆ 50cm/20in ⬌ 50cm/20in   EASY

A slow-growing, rounded, fully hardy evergreen conifer from North America, with a neat habit and flattened upright branches of emerald green aromatic foliage, bronzed at the tips; insignificant, nugget-like tan cones are produced in autumn to winter.

Thuja occidentalis 'Holmstrup'
White cedar

⬆ 4m/13ft ⬌ 1.5m/5ft   EASY

A slow-growing (up to 20cm/8in a year), upright, conical, fully hardy evergreen conifer from North America, with dense, dark green upright sprays of flattened, scaly, aromatic needles, and small, smooth, oval brown cones. Deer proof.

Thuja occidentalis 'Sunkist'

⬆ 1.5m/5ft ⬌ 90cm/3ft   EASY

A slow-growing, pyramid-shaped, fully hardy evergreen conifer from North America, with pineapple-scented, golden yellow foliage in summer, flushed orange at the tips in winter, and small, pale rose-coloured cones.

THUJOPSIS

A group of slow-growing, **fully hardy** evergreen coniferous trees from Japanese woodlands that are similar to *Thuja* but tend to have larger leaves and broader branches, with brown bark. The dwarf varieties are best for smaller spaces. Grow in moist, well-drained soil in full sun, with shelter from the wind.

Thujopsis dolabrata 'Aurea'

↑ 1.2m/4ft ↔ 80cm/32in   EASY

A slow-growing, bushy, pyramid-shaped, fully hardy evergreen conifer from Japan, with flat sprays of glossy green foliage, suffused with gold, and silver-marked undersides; attractive, reddish-brown bark peels away in papery layers, and scaly brown cones are produced from autumn.

Thujopsis dolabrata 'Nana'

↑ 90cm/3ft ↔ 80cm/32in   EASY

A dwarf, fully hardy evergreen conifer from Japan that makes a neat, compact, flat-topped dome of shiny emerald green leaves in flattened sprays, tipped brown in winter; small oval cones ripen to brown over two to three years.

Trachycarpus fortunei ♛ Chusan palm

↑ 12m/40ft ↔ 2.5m/8ft   MEDIUM

A slow-growing, architectural, frost-hardy evergreen palm from Asia that will only reach its ultimate height after many decades, and grows even more slowly (about 15cm/6in per year, on average) in colder climates. It has a matted, hairy, red to grey single trunk made up of old fibrous leaf stems, and large, fan-shaped, leathery, deep green leaves; rather ordinary clusters of yellow flowers in summer are followed by rounded blue-black berries. It will thrive in any well-drained soil, in full sun or partial shade, with protection from winds; it is easy to grow in the right climate and it becomes more frost tolerant with age, so protect young trees from excessive cold or freezing in their first few years. Can be grown in large pots in towns, or in an exotic or desert-style garden.

TSUGA Hemlock

This group of elegant, spreading, evergreen coniferous trees, found across Asia to North America, is similar to *Taxus* in appearance, with short, flat, linear leaves on branching, drooping branches. The smaller forms often grow wider than they are tall, making excellent ground cover. If grown as hedging, clip in spring and late summer. Grow in any moist, well-drained, humus-rich soil, with shelter from cold or drying winds.

Tsuga canadensis 'Cole's Prostrate'

↑ 30cm/12in ↔ 90cm/3ft   EASY

A very slow-growing, spreading, dwarf, fully hardy evergreen conifer from North America, with dense, graceful, cascading, weeping branches with mid-green needles, almost at ground level, pale greyish bark, and small, oval, pale brown pendent cones. Makes excellent ground cover.

Tsuga canadensis 'Jeddeloh' ♛
Bird's nest hemlock (below)

↑ 50cm/20in ↔ 90cm/3ft   EASY

A reliable, rounded, spreading, dwarf, fully hardy evergreen conifer from North America, with tiered, slightly arching, low-growing branches of bright green needled leaves, with white markings underneath, and small, oval, pendent brown cones.

Tsuga canadensis 'Pendula' ♛

↑ 4m/13ft ↔ 8m/26ft   EASY

A slow-growing, weeping, fully hardy evergreen conifer from North America, forming an architectural draped mound of overlapping, slightly drooping branches, clothed in deep green needles, and small, sturdy, green cones from autumn.

Planting with evergreen plants

Evergreens are incredibly versatile, lending their enduring foliage to a wide variety of planting styles. Some are tall and showy, delivering great vertical lines, while others have a carpeting nature, making them ideal as ground cover. Evergreen trees and shrubs may be grown as individual specimens in lawns and borders, or gathered together to form hedges, providing shelter and privacy. These are plants with purpose – and many also have flowers, fragrance or berries as icing on the cake for the adventurous gardener.

Hedges act as boundary devices, ensure privacy from our neighbours, screen us from traffic noise, add architectural lines, create divisions in the garden and provide camouflage for unsightly areas. They also provide a safe haven for nesting birds and wildlife. A hedge that is intended to act as a screen, windbreak or boundary will be tall and cast shade; small hedges may be used as edging or be entirely ornamental. Whatever your reason for growing a hedge, choose your plant material wisely as it is going to be a permanent feature in the garden.

Decide whether your hedge is to be formal (using dense, uniform, non-flowering evergreen plants) or informal (using flowering evergreen shrubs). The majority of us plant hedges using only one variety of plant, but planting mixed hedging is another option.

When choosing boundary hedges, look for plants that have a manageable growth rate, and think about how much maintenance you can handle. There are many magnificent evergreen trees and shrubs with appealing leaf textures and perhaps flowers or berries that will provide generous screening within three years. If you feel you cannot wait, specialist nurseries will supply mature shrubs. It is quite possible to buy an established hedge 2m/6ft high or a tree of 3m/10ft (or more), though naturally they will cost a good deal more than young plants. Don't be tempted to plant fast-growing conifers: these are often dull-looking and will soon get out of hand.

If a neighbour's garden is involved, a consultation about what to plant will

LEFT *Photinia* x *fraseri* 'Red Robin' makes an attractive evergreen hedge

prevent unpleasantness later. Hedges need cutting on both sides, so a neighbourly willingness to participate in the upkeep is an advantage. It is mean-spirited to plant *leylandii* on a neighbour's boundary when it will soon block the available sunlight. This book gives you plenty of choices. Be nice and plant something else. Just pop in some fast-growing climbers to give instant screening while you are waiting for the hedge to grow.

In coastal areas or exposed parts of the country, plants can be thrashed by harsh winds. Grown as windbreaks, hedges and trees provide sanctuary against raw weather. Planting a stout, tough hedge, such as berberis, griselinia or escallonia in the path of the prevailing winds is one of the quickest methods of achieving a shelter belt. With this protection, plants can establish without being buffeted or stunted by cruel weather. (If you're patient and have a large garden, you may opt for an ornamental layered windbreak, using pines, larch or spruce and mixed shrubs, such as choisya or gorse (*Ulex europaeus*), to bear the brunt of the wind.)

Many plants can be used as informal low hedging, including cotoneasters, some of the larger euphorbias, lavender, rosemary and santolina. Box is faster-growing than most people give it credit for and forms a slick, tight, formal low hedging. As an alternative, *Lonicera nitida* will form a respectable low hedge within three years (but it will need more frequent clipping than box).

Left to their own devices, many hedges would naturally grow into trees, but cutting them back every year ensures they do not reach their full size. For taller hedging, yew and holly or the hugely popular Portuguese and cherry laurels are the norm, but other plants will adapt happily to the task. Consider growing choisya or elaeagnus for their scent, photinia, with its red-tinted young foliage, or escallonia, which has pink-white apple blossom blooms.

Evergreen trees and shrubs make ideal specimens in borders, lawns or containers. Choose something that has an attractive shape and won't overpower existing plants. When planting in a border, avoid shrubs with dense foliage, which cuts out light, or those that drink heavily from the soil, to the disadvantage of other greenery. *Garrya elliptica* makes an elegant focal plant without handicapping its neighbours, and viburnums are fabulous as sculptural half-standards, with super glossy leaves as well as pretty pink flowers in late winter.

Topiary comes into its own here. Visit a topiary specialist and you will see a huge array of sculpted greenery that offers instant visual impact. You can choose from traditional box balls, bay pyramids, spiralling conifers, cloud-pruned hollies, pillared camellias, cylinder cedars, privet lollipops and honeysuckled hearts, lavender horns and hens! These are likely to be pricey but are worthwhile investments in the long term, offering creative punctuation to your garden.

Some evergreen trees attain great heights and are only suitable for very large gardens, but there are beautiful trees that can be grown in smaller spaces, such as *Abies koreana* 'Silberlocke' or *Arbutus unedo* 'Compacta'. Planting small trees and shrubs in large pots and containers is one way to limit their size. And some trees are so slow-growing that they are unlikely to cause problems for many years, if at all. Take time when choosing a tree. If you have a tiny city garden, don't plant a potential whopper that will fill the space with shade and may undermine paving, building foundations and drains once its roots go searching for water.

Many people are better acquainted with coniferous trees than with evergreen shrubs and perennials, and conifers certainly do a sterling job in terms of foliage, architectural shapes and screening. (Coniferous trees and large-leaved evergreen shrubs can also make very effective sound-proofing, absorbing and muffling ambient traffic noise.) And some conifers are outstanding ornamental trees. These include the imposing and decorative *Cedrus atlantica* Glauca Group 'Glauca Pendula'.

Evergreen climbers are invaluable in small gardens, where space is limited, and wall-climbing shrubs such as cotoneaster, euonymus and pyracantha also have a part to play. The Chilean bellfower (*Lapageria rosea*) offers year-long foliage with pendulous rosy pink flowers from summer to autumn. And there is a list of ivies as long as your arm that will provide a splash of colour in gloomy corners with their brightening variegated foliage and architectural flower umbels.

As well as disguising unsightly features, evergreen plants are indispensable for covering ground, particularly when it is difficult to cultivate. You only have to look at our obsession with lawns to see what impact all those tiny grasses make, giving us swards of green – and what is grass if not year-round evergreen ground cover? Low-growing carpeting plants are the obvious choice as ground cover, but many larger plants, such as grasses, ferns and small shrubs, are fabulous when planted in multiples, giving more unusual, visually stimulating low-level coverage.

Every garden has problem areas where few plants will thrive. These include the dry, shady ground under tree canopies or in the shadow of neighbouring buildings. Most evergreens are pretty tolerant of shade and need little maintenance, so they are perfect planting solutions for these difficult spots. Vinca, pachysandra and low-growing evergreen shrubs such as skimmia and

sarcococca provide reliable covering for earthy patches. Ivies also make terrific ground cover (but don't plant the megalomaniac common ivy in town gardens: it's far too rampant and is no respecter of boundaries or dodgy brickwork).

For anyone lucky enough to have a garden with sunny aspects, there are sun-loving evergreens that will happily cover the ground. *Festuca glauca*, rock roses (*Cistus*), heathers (*Calluna*) and hebes all provide elegant ground cover which lasts into autumn and through winter, when there is a dearth of textural foliage.

Planning an evergreen garden

Let us imagine that you have a typically long, narrow, bare town garden. There are a couple of sorry-looking brown fence panels between you and your neighbours, and the garden is overshadowed by tall buildings. A sensible approach would be to add some (not all) evergreenness, for year-round interest. You don't want anything too large or spreading that will cut out the sun, so a small tree or large shrub, with foliage that is not too dense and hopefully some form of flower, might be an ideal starting point.

One of the small azaras will offer scent and flower, while a modestly growing myrtle (*Myrtus*) has great foliage, bark and white flower blossoms. Viburnums grow reasonably quickly and can be left as large specimen shrubs or easily trained into half-standards. Cordylines, phormiums or Chusan palms (*Trachycarpus fortunei*) will give a more tropical feel. Select a few key evergreen trees and/or shrubs and plant these as your garden wallpaper. They will always be on show, forming a permanent green structure.

Now pick a mixture of smaller shrubs, climbers and perennials to furnish your outdoor room, choosing from hypericums, scented choisyas and bold, colourful blooming rhododendrons, for example. A lush sward of lawn may be your preferred choice of evergreen carpeting, with shorter perennials starring alongside as low-level focal points.

A contemporary garden scheme could use architectural plants such as ferns and grasses, phormiums and euphorbias. Grasses make a very definite green clump of upright habit, which gives excellent vertical contrast to mounding or spreading plants and offers interesting focal points throughout the year. Added to this you could artfully employ some topiary, with textured foliage provided by box (*Buxus*), fatsia, holly (*Ilex*), shrubby honeysuckle (*Lonicera*) and viburnum; even rosemary and lavender can be sculpted to form modern formal shapes.

If you plant a large number of small-leaved plants, everything in the garden will look very 'samey', so choose some plants with larger leaf sizes too and consider how the leaf shapes will complement one another. Plants with red-tinted leaves in spring or autumn, such as ajuga, bergenia or pieris, are also very effective in lifting the uniformity of an all-green palette.

Additionally there are many beautiful silver-leaved evergreen plants. Lavender, honeysuckle and thrift (*Armeria*) all blend perfectly with cottage garden planting, and a sunny paved area presents an ideal opportunity to create a drought-busting Mediterranean-style garden. Silver-foliaged plants enjoy full sun and well-drained soil, and they do very well in pots, so they can be highly effective in courtyards and on balconies, and are natural contenders for sunny window boxes and containers.

Growing trees and shrubs that produce autumn and winter berries is a great way of extending interest in the garden and

ABOVE *Vinca minor* 'Atropurpurea' provides excellent cover for earthy patches

ensuring it is a friendly place for foraging birds. However, berrying shrubs often have male and female flowers on different plants, so you may need to grow one of each to achieve the pollination that will result in vivid berry displays.

A garden with a complement of evergreen planting is always going to look good in winter. When all those fair-weather herbaceous perennials lie shivering under the soil, evergreens stand unflinching and resplendent, adorning the garden with varied, textured foliage and, very often, winter flowers and berries. Be creative and bold in your choices and you will end up with a garden that pleases the eye every single day of the year.

Aspect

Sun and shade

When choosing plants, it is important to know how much sunlight your garden enjoys, and which areas are prone to shade. All plants need direct or indirect sunlight to survive, but the amount of sun they need varies enormously. Some plants will sulk in anything other than full sun, while others are happier in partial or full shade.

The direction your garden faces is referred to as its aspect. East-facing beds will be in sun most of the morning, south-facing beds in sun all day and those facing west may get the afternoon and evening sun. North-facing gardens get the least light of all and have a tendency to dampness; woodland or shade-loving plants do better in these situations.

Tall trees or large buildings overlooking the garden can cast even a sunny garden into shade, and garden sheds, garages and outbuildings may create shady patches. Notice your garden's cooler spots and take time to see where the light is throughout the day and at different times of year.

Where you have a choice, site beds against west or south-facing walls or fences; this will give the widest range of options for growing plants. North-facing beds are notorious trouble spots, but shade-loving plants and plants with large leaves will usually thrive in these gloomier conditions; plants that will be happy on a north-facing wall include roses and climbers (although flowering will be reduced). The vast majority of evergreen shrubs will tolerate these conditions.

The plant descriptions give plants' preferences for facing north, east, south or west. Plants that originally come from the Mediterranean or other warm climes are used to long hours of sunshine and are more likely to succeed in a southerly or west-facing spot.

Most other evergreens are not particularly fussy about aspect, but they may need careful siting to get the best from them in terms of foliage colour and flower production. Place your garden plants in their preferred aspect and they will grow well for you.

Shelter

Brick walls, fencing and hedges or mature trees and shrubs all create shelter (see page 91), absorbing the worst of the weather and protecting your plants. Gardens without shelter take the full force of cold winds, hard rain, frosts and snow in winter, and drying winds and direct overhead sunlight in the summer months.

Wind can do a surprising amount of damage, leading to scorching or loss of foliage, preventing your plant attaining its true potential. If a tree, shrub or perennial needs protection from wind, plant it where there is a buffer against the elements, near a fence or wall, or use house walls, garages and outbuildings to act as wind deflectors.

Frosts are not much of an issue for gardeners in mild areas and city centres, but in colder regions hard frosts in winter and into spring are a regular hazard. Most of the plants in this book are fully hardy and need no protection beyond the shelter of a garden environment. A wall that enjoys long hours of sunshine will have warm soil at its footings and rarely be exposed to any winds, providing an ideal micro-climate. Every garden has a sheltered corner somewhere, and prudent gardeners should utilise these weather refuges wherever possible. Use horticultural fleece, old sacking or bubblewrap to protect plants that are less hardy, or overwinter them in frost-free comfort in a greenhouse.

Soil

Most plants need soil to grow: it anchors them firmly into the ground and provides the nutrients, air and water that they need. Different plants prefer different soils and the type and quality of soil is a major factor in growing any plant successfully. With a few notable exceptions, evergreen tress and shrubs loathe waterlogged soils. Unless the profile specifies that a plant enjoys boggy ground, avoid sodden soil at all costs. A good soil is:

- **moist** – able to retain water, without becoming boggy
- **fertile** – rich in nutrients and able to support new plant growth
- **well-drained** – allowing excess surface water to drain away
- **crumbly and open in texture** – allowing roots to grow through it easily

Types of soil

There are four common types of garden soil: sandy, clay, loam and chalk. These vary in their ability to retain water, their nutrient values and their acidity or alkalinity.

Sandy soil is light, dry, well-aerated soil that is free draining and easy to dig. Because water drains through very quickly and nutrients are easily washed away, sandy soil needs enriching with organic matter to improve water retention and fertility (unless you are growing plants that like poor conditions, such as silver-leaved Mediterranean plants and others from similar climates: these will thrive in unimproved sandy soil).

Clay soils are wet and heavy to dig in winter but rock hard in times of drought. The soil texture is heavy and condensed, and aeration is poor, so many plants struggle to get their roots down into clay. It is slow to warm up in spring, but retains warmth well once the growing season is under way. Clay soil is high in nutrients and supports a wider selection of plants than any other soil, with the exception of loam. Most evergreen trees prefer well-drained soil, but will be happy enough in clay so long as it is not waterlogged. If in doubt, dig in some horticultural grit and organic matter when planting.

Loam is rich, dark brown in colour, helping it absorb the heat of the sun, with a crumbly texture. It combines all the good points of clay and sandy soil, without any of the disadvantages. It is easy to dig, has high nutrient levels, good water retention and, because of its friable composition, plant roots establish easily. Most plants in this book will thrive in loam.

Chalk (or limestone) soils are very free draining, so they lack fertility as nutrients are washed away. They can be parched in summer and sticky and difficult to dig in winter. Adding organic matter is the only reliable method of improving chalky soils. There are many lime-hating plants, so planting choices can be limited; plants that are happy in chalky soils include arbutus, aucuba, berberis, ceanothus and cistus.

Soil **acidity** or **alkalinity** can affect your choice of plants. It is measured by the soil's pH value, on a scale of 1–14; soil with a pH of 7 is said to be neutral, below 7 is acid and above 7 is alkaline (simple soil testing kits are easily available). Most plants will grow in soil with a pH between 6 and 7, but some plants are acid-lovers and can't thrive in neutral soils; these are known as ericaceous plants and they include camellias, ericas, pieris, pines and rhododendrons. Avoid them if you have neutral or alkaline soil.

Improving the soil

Most gardeners don't have perfect soil. However, whether your soil is heavy and waterlogged or as dry as dust, you can make it easier to work with and provide a better growing environment for your plants.

Adding bulky organic matter, such as well-rotted manure, leafmould or garden compost, to the soil improves its aeration and fertility, which in turn aids good root growth and seed germination. It also helps the soil to retain water, as organic matter acts like a sponge.

Feeding the soil with organic matter reduces the need to use foliar fertilisers. Chemical tonics will give plants a short-term boost if they are looking a little yellow or are growing poorly, but they do not improve the structure or fertility of the soil and are not a substitute for organic matter.

Digging in horticultural grit or small-sized gravel is invaluable for heavy clay soils that are waterlogged or compacted. It opens up the soil, allowing roots, water and air to penetrate more freely and improving drainage.

As a general guide, do the following in late winter or early spring:

- **sandy soil** – dig in organic matter
- **clay soil** – dig in grit; dig in organic matter or spread it on the surface
- **compacted soil** – dig in grit, and organic matter if needed; rotovate to break up the compacted surface layer
- **wet soil** – dig in grit or gravel; if the soil is very wet, consider digging soakaways, ditches or drains, or plant in raised beds

Do this every year for three or four years and the condition of your soil will improve enormously. Once the soil is in a workable condition, you can adopt a more leisurely regime, adding organic matter to your beds or at the base of trees, shrubs and perennials every two or three years. Easy.

Organic soil improvers

As plants grow, they draw on nitrogen in the soil. Dead leaves, plant debris and lawn trimmings break down to replenish the nitrogen supplies, but we interrupt this process by tidying our gardens. Organic soil improvers replace this lost material.

Farmyard manure is available in garden centres, or from animal owners in rural areas. It must be well rotted (black, and with little or no smell) or it can scorch or kill your plants.

Apply it in autumn or late winter on clay soil or in early spring for sandy soils. If the soil is very heavy, compacted or waterlogged, dig it into the top 30cm/12in in the first year. Otherwise, spread a thick layer (5–8cm/2–3in) over the beds and let nature do the work.

Mushroom compost is light and easy to use. It contains chalk (which is alkaline) and is useful for acid soils, which tend to have poor fertility.

Apply as a mulch, spreading a generous layer (5–8cm/2–3in deep) on the soil (20kg/44lb will cover 1sq m/1sq yd) in autumn on clay soil or late winter or early spring for sandy soils. Don't use mushroom compost to mulch plants that are acid-lovers. If you are gardening on alkaline, neutral or chalky soil, only use mushroom compost every three years or so: continuous use can result in excessive alkalinity.

Leafmould (rotted leaves) is rich in humus, beneficial bacteria and micro-organisms. It adds bulk to the soil and improves its texture. To make leafmould, rake fallen leaves together and put in a wire mesh bin or black bin liners, keeping them separate from other compost as they take longer to rot down. Water them if they are dry and leave for a year or two.

Dig in leafmould to bulk up sandy soil and open up clay soil. Use leafmould that is at least two years old and very well-rotted for potting plants and seed-sowing: mix it with equal parts of sharp sand, loam and garden compost.

Green waste soil improver is a coarse-textured material made from domestic waste that has been composted by local authorities. Use it to improve soil structure.

Garden compost is plant matter that has been collected from the garden and left to decay. It is an efficient, free way of recycling plant waste and adds bulk and nutrients to the soil.

Any plant matter will compost eventually but brown, woody material takes longer to break down than green, non-woody material. When making compost, it is important to get

ABOVE Collecting autumn leaves for leafmould

the right balance of ingredients, using roughly equal amounts of green and brown plant material. Avoid substances that don't break down (ashes, tins) or attract vermin (food).

Green material includes spent bedding plants, soft green non-woody prunings, grass clippings and vegetable peelings, as well as coffee grounds or teabags: these all rot quickly. Don't add diseased plants or perennial weeds such as dandelions, bindweed and buttercups. Nettles are the exception: being very nitrogenous, they speed up the decaying process.

Brown material includes cardboard, crushed eggshells, shredded paper, straw, tough hedge clippings and sawdust. Woody material bulks up the finished compost but is slow to decay (chop or shred it to speed up the process). Fallen leaves decay very slowly, and are better used to make leafmould.

Site compost bins or heaps directly on the soil or grass in a corner of the garden in full sun or partial shade. They need a lid or cover; an old piece of carpet works well.

MAKING COMPOST

There are two ways to make compost: a 'hot' heap is made from a large amount of material which is left to heat up and is ready to use within months; a 'cool' heap is built up in layers as material becomes available and takes a year or so to decay.

Hot heaps Make a thick base layer of woody plants or twigs to aid air circulation and drainage. Fill the bin or build the heap with well-mixed green and brown material, watering as you go. Cover and leave to heat up. Turn the heap after a couple of weeks, mixing well, and add water if it has dried out. Leave for some months until it reaches the desired texture: it should smell earthy, not dank and rotten, and be dark brown and crumbly (don't worry about the odd lump or twig).

Cool heaps Start with a base layer as above, add a 40cm/16in layer of mixed composting material, and cover. Add further layers as material becomes available. Check after a year. If the top layer has not broken down but the bottom is ready, take out the finished compost and mix the drier, less decayed material back into the heap; add water, cover and wait a few months more.

Growing

The evergreen plants in this book range from small perennials to shrubs and trees, and they have varying needs for sun and shade, soil and water. In general, evergreen plants suffer a lot less from diseases and pests than other plants (this is especially true of the species with aromatic foliage), and they usually need very little maintenance. Evergreen plants keep their leaves all year round, unlike deciduous trees or herbaceous perennials, which lose their leaves or die back at the end of the growing season.

Evergreen perennials may have tuberous, rhizomatous, taprooted or fibrous roots; there are some bulbous evergreens, but these are not included in this book. They are usually hardy and need little maintenance. (Tender evergreens that come from warm climates can't cope with low temperatures and frost. Since these are not evergreen in our climate, they are also not included.)

Evergreen grasses are also perennials. They need a tidy-up in spring: comb your fingers through to remove any dead or damaged growth and diseased foliage or snip out tatty growth with secateurs. Otherwise, they need no maintenance.

Semi-evergreen perennials may lose some leaves in cold winters and their leaves can look a little tatty by year's end, but this is easily remedied by cutting off the dishevelled foliage. They may need protecting with dry ferns, straw, fleece or bubblewrap in winter.

Evergreen climbers are simply plants that climb. They include perennials and wall shrubs. For the most part, they need little or no pruning, but they do need support (see page 102).

Evergreen trees and shrubs retain their foliage through all the seasons. They are reliable, low-maintenance plants once established, but they need some nursing through their first three formative years. After that, shrubs will need occasional light pruning, and hedges will need cutting.

Buying

Evergreen perennials, including climbers and grasses, are usually sold in pots. They can be kept in their pots for up to a year as long as they are well watered.

It is tempting to buy large plants that will have more impact, but small plants are just fine: they establish better and you have the pleasure of seeing them grow. Unlikely as it may seem, young perennials will achieve a good height and spread within a year. Big is not necessarily best.

Look for a well-balanced plant, and always buy plants in good health. It is far better to choose a smaller plant with really healthy-looking foliage than something larger with yellowing patches on the leaves. If the plant is not too big, up-end it into your hand: the roots should be white and healthy and not wrapping themselves round in circles. Press your thumb into the surface of the compost to see it is moist and spongy. Roots escaping through the bottom of the pot and compost that is dry or contains weeds are signs of neglect: walk on by.

Evergreen shrubs come in all sizes, from small container-grown plants to semi-mature specimens supplied in huge, heavy pots (which will be a lot more expensive). They can also be bought as bare-root plants or rootballs.

Bare-root plants are dug up with only a small amount of soil on their roots. They come with a strong root and main and side stems, but they are relatively young plants

evergreen

and don't have the bushiness or density of a rootballed or mature container-grown plant. Rootballed plants are dug up to order, with their rootball intact and wrapped in biodegradable hessian sacking. Both are available in the dormant season, from November to March.

It is much cheaper to buy hedging plants as bare-root or rootballed plants from specialist nurseries, rather than buying pot-grown plants. Bare-root plants are usually sold in standard sizes, such as 30–40cm (12–16in), 40–60cm (16–24in) or 60–80cm (24–32in), and are ideal for a long run of hedging that is uniform in height and girth. Look for bushy plants that have good coverage from just above the bottom of the stem.

When purchasing shrubs (including wall shrubs) it is especially important to choose a well-balanced plant that is not top-heavy, with evenly spaced stems or branches. Check that the leaves are free from damage, scorch or disease, and the stems are undamaged.

Evergreen trees are available in various sizes, ranging from small seedlings to semi-

ABOVE Your local garden centre is a good place to stock up on evergreen plants

mature specimens and may be bought container-grown, bare root or rootballed. Choose a tree that has a straight trunk, with an even spread of branches. Check the leaves are green, healthy and disease free.

Where to buy? There are so many places to buy good-quality plants. Garden centres are the obvious place to find plants locally, and specialist nurseries with mail order or online facilities offer unusual plants and a wider choice of varieties than is normally available, and they are generous about giving cultivation advice. Bare-root and rootballed plants are available from specialists (look in the *RHS Plant Finder* for relevant nurseries). Nurserymen and women have a wealth of knowledge that they are happy to share, so don't be shy about asking for guidance. And you can often find plants at markets and garden open days, or beg cuttings from friends.

Planting

Choose a place that has the right aspect and soil for your plant. Some plants dislike cold or drying winds, so provide them with a sheltered spot, but remember that the earth at the bottom of walls is notoriously dry, and may have concrete footings; plant climbers 30–90cm/12–36in away from the wall and angle the plant towards it. Try not to plant trees too close to buildings and other structures such as walls and paths. Bear in mind how large a tree or shrub is likely to grow and leave sufficient space.

Container-grown plants can be planted at any time of year, though autumn to spring is ideal (most plants do better if planted in October when the soil is still warm). Avoid planting if the ground is dry, frozen or waterlogged, and keep plants well watered when planting in summer.

Plants appreciate a good drink before planting. Give them a thorough soaking or dunk them in a bucket of water for half an hour, so the water really saturates the roots.

Dig a hole about the same size as the pot, with enough space to accommodate the roots easily, and break up the soil in the bottom of the planting hole, as this helps the roots to establish. Add a handful of garden compost or well-rotted manure to the planting hole, unless the plants are silver-leaved (in which case, add a handful of grit to the planting hole, to give really sharp drainage).

Turn the plant upside down, cupping the foliage with your hand for support, and gently ease the plant from the pot, taking care not to disturb the rootball too much. Container-grown plants often have roots that are wrapped in circles: gently tease them apart and spread them in the planting hole. Position the plant so that the compost is level with the surrounding soil.

If the weather is dry and you haven't had time to water the plant beforehand, place it in the planting hole and puddle it in by pouring several litres of water into the hole and letting it drain away before backfilling with soil.

Firm the plant down really well with your hands after backfilling, and water again. This ensures the roots make good contact with the soil. Apply a ring of organic matter (about 5cm/2in thick) around the base of the plant after planting.

Bare-root and rootballed plants are planted between November and March, when they are not in active growth. It is important to plant evergreens into their final positions as soon as possible after delivery: although they are dormant, they are still supporting foliage and their roots need protecting.

If you have to delay planting bare-root plants, dig a trench and place the plants in it, spreading the roots and soaking them in water before roughly backfilling the trench with soil. Water the foliage lightly, unless the weather is freezing, and plant as soon as possible.

Water any rootballed plants that you cannot plant immediately and cover them with further sacking or bubblewrap to protect the roots from drying out or being frosted. Better still, group them together on the ground and shovel earth over the rootballs until they can be planted. Again, plant on as soon as possible.

Plant individual plants as described above for container-grown plants. The planting hole should be as wide and as deep as the rootball, so that it is planted level with the soil surface. Don't plant shrubs and trees too deep, as this can prevent them establishing well.

To ensure new trees grow straight and strong, support them with a stake (see

PLANTING A HEDGE

Trees, conifers or shrubs planted close together in a line form a hedge. This is usually clipped about three times a year, to restrict its size and height.

You can opt to make a hedge from a single or double row of plants, depending on your needs. Double-row hedges are more likely to be stock proof and will provide more efficient shelter than single-row hedging; they will also be broader when mature, which makes them more difficult to maintain. Hedges can be allowed to grow tall enough to ensure privacy or shelter, grown as shorter decorative garden divisions or as dwarf hedging.

Bare-root hedging plants usually come tied together in bundles of 25–30 plants. Dunk the entire bundle in water for a couple of hours to soak the roots before planting. Water container-grown and rootballed plants either before planting or once they are in the planting hole.

Weed the planting area thoroughly and peg a string along the planting line. Dig holes (or a trench if you are planting a lot of bare-root plants, as you can space them more evenly) in front of your string line, just a bit wider than the root spread and one and a half times the depth. When planting rootballs or container-grown plants, make the hole slightly wider than the pot, so you can manoeuvre it into the hole, and easily as deep as the pot or rootball.

The distances between individual plants will vary according to their initial size and how long you are prepared to wait for the gaps to fill out. As a rough rule of thumb, evergreen hedging plants are usually spaced 60–90cm/2–3ft apart. Smaller plants, such as bare-root box, can be planted closer together (20–50cm/8–20in apart) but you will still need to leave space between plants to allow for future growth and good air circulation. Seek advice from the nursery about planting numbers and distances for specific plants. They will be delighted to help.

In unseasonably wet weather, trenches or holes may fill with water and need draining before you can plant. Line the hole or trench with some well-rotted manure or add a general-purpose fertiliser, forking it in lightly. Place each plant in the hole, spreading the roots out gently and ensuring the plants are evenly spaced (one out of line now will look even more wrongly placed as the plants mature).

Puddle in container-grown and rootballed plants, filling the holes with a few litres of water and waiting until the water drains away completely before backfilling the hole. (When planting hedging, I backfill with a combination of the dug-out soil and well-rotted manure.) Keep the plants upright and straight and ensure that the base of the stems is not buried, as this can cause plants to rot. Tread down firmly with the heel of your boot the base of the soil around each plant.

If you soaked the plant roots before planting, there is no need to water them again immediately after planting. However, I always water both before and after planting, especially if the weather has been excessively dry or on free-draining sandy soil.

Keep new hedges weed free at the base and water regularly in the growing season for the first year or two, particularly in dry spells, and mulch with organic matter.

Pruning and clipping Immediately after planting, prune away any straggly side stems. In the first year or two trim lightly in May, to encourage bushy growth. Repeat this every year until your hedge has reached the right height.

Clip hedges between May and August, to keep the foliage tight and dense. This may need doing as little as once a year, or as much as every six to eight weeks for formal hedging such as privet. Once the plants have reached their desired height, clip as necessary to maintain height and spread.

page 103). If rabbits and deer are a problem, wrap protective tree guards around the trunks, to prevent animals stripping the bark.

Water the tree immediately after planting, and keep it regularly watered in the first three summers, after which it should be able to take care of itself. Once planted, there is no need to prune or cut back either evergreen trees or shrubs unless you are growing a hedge (see above).

Remember to mulch round the base of the tree every spring as part of your annual garden maintenance, to keep weeds at bay and to feed it.

Supporting plants

Climbers almost always need support. Some are unable to support their mature weight, while others need something to cling to.

Many gardeners underestimate the weight of a fully clothed mature evergreen plant. Spindly structures that seemed more than adequate at the time of planting tend to buckle as the plant grows heavier and wider. Make provision for a plant's ultimate size and weight from the outset.

A few climbers are self-clinging. For example, ivy has small aerial roots with which it can cling to almost any rough surface (and they are strong enough to damage masonry and crumbling brick mortar joints). Other climbing plants need assistance to climb. They can be grown on trellis or wires attached to walls and fences, or up sturdy free-standing structures such as pillars and pergolas, arbours and archways. Always use soft string or garden twine when tying

ABOVE Planting in pots is a great way to showcase evergreen shrubs such as *Pieris* 'Forest Flame'

CONTAINER PLANTING

Evergreen shrubs and trees can be planted in containers and placed as focal points in the garden. Topiary (see box on page 106) is often used in this way. When planting in containers:

- choose frost-proof pots
- lay crocks at the bottom over the drainage holes
- use a good multi-purpose compost or homemade garden compost, but don't use old compost
- mix water-swelling granules with the compost, to reduce the need for constant watering
- cover the soil surface with a layer of leafmould, mushroom compost, decorative gravel or bark to reduce water evaporation

Plants in pots dry out much more quickly than those planted in the ground. Water generously when necessary (this could be every other day but, if you have used water granules, once a week should be sufficient) and ensure the water is soaking through to

the roots. The compost should feel damp to the touch, but not waterlogged. Sometimes the compost gets a dry cap or crust, preventing water reaching the roots: a drop of washing-up liquid in the watering can will break the surface tension.

Plants in containers soon use up the nutrients in their limited portion of soil, so top up the pot each year with about 5cm/2in of fresh compost or soil and use slow-release fertiliser pellets or apply an annual liquid feed. Pull up any weeds as you spot them.

Container plants are particularly susceptible to vine weevil (see page 111), so check pots regularly. A drench that will treat and prevent vine weevil infestations is available from garden centres.

It may be necessary to move plants into a larger pot every three years or so. Once you see roots straggling through the hole at the pot bottom, you know the plant is feeling cramped. It is time to transfer it to a slightly larger pot.

climbing plants to supports, whether trellis or wire, to prevent damage to the plant.

When fixing trellis, mount it on wooden battens to create a gap between the trellis and the wall: this ensures good air circulation around the plant, which will help to reduce the potential for disease.

Alternatively, attach galvanised or plastic-coated wires to fencing or walls using vine eyes or tension bolts, placed no more than 2m/6ft apart. Fix the first horizontal wire 45cm/18in above ground level, which is low enough to allow the climber to attach itself to the support. Position further wires 30–45cm/12–18in apart, threading the wires through the vine eyes and using a pair of pliers to stretch them taut before tying them off securely. Make the framework of wires larger than you need, to allow for growth in future years. If you are securing wires along panelled fencing, fix the wires to the fence posts using galvanised staples.

Trees and shrubs are generally self-supporting, but young trees need staking for the first few years after planting. Bang the tree stake in firmly, without driving it through the tree roots, and use a rubber tie to secure the tree firmly to the stake. The stake should be about one third the height of the tree. Remove the stake and tie after two to three years.

Wall shrubs can be bought trained against a caned framework, but it is easy to tie them in to trellis or wires as they grow, if they need support (see above). Prune out any stems that grow out of line.

Mulching

Organic or inorganic materials placed on the soil or around the base of plants are known as mulches. They help prevent moisture loss from the soil and stop weeds growing.

Organic mulches also help soil to retain water and improve soil fertility.

Never mulch dry or frozen ground. Ensure the soil is moist or give it a thorough watering before mulching. To mulch perennials, shrubs and trees, spread a 5–8cm/2–3in layer of organic matter, either on the surface of beds or around the base of plants, annually in early spring. Plants that like woodland conditions or need reliably moist soil will particularly appreciate being mulched with leafmould.

TYPES OF MULCH

Organic mulches include the organic soil improvers – well-rotted manure, leafmould, mushroom compost or garden compost (see pages 96–7) – that are essential to garden health. Mulching with these

- increases the soil's fertility
- improves the soil's ability to retain water
- traps moisture at plants' roots, where it can be taken up more effectively
- reduces water evaporation from the soil surface
- suppresses weeds by blocking out light to weed seed
- helps the soil absorb the sun's warmth, which leads to good root establishment

Some organic mulches do not improve the soil: cocoa shells and ornamental bark rob nitrogen from the soil while they are breaking down. They can be decorative and will suppress weeds but are not soil conditioners.

Inorganic mulches such as gravel or granite chippings reduce water loss and keep weeds down, but they do not feed the soil and are essentially decorative.

Dry mulches include natural materials such as dried leaves, old fern fronds or straw as well as horticultural fleece and bubblewrap. These are used to protect vulnerable plants when temperatures fall. Tuck the mulch around the base of the plants or place about 10cm/4in of material on top of the plant (the crown) and firm it down gently. This will give protection from snowfall, frost and wet.

Watering

It is important to preserve water in the soil and use available water as efficiently as possible. Improving the soil's ability to retain moisture by increasing its organic content is the first line of defence in water conservation, and is one reason why mulching with organic matter is so important.

Water in the early hours of the morning or in late evening, when there is less risk of wastage from evaporation, about three times a week. Water slowly, thoroughly and generously. Generous watering encourages plants (and lawns) to root deeply. Watering with a small amount of water or too frequently can lead to plants making shallow roots near the surface. Shallow-rooted plants are the first to keel over in dry periods.

Large gardens can take hours to water properly, so think about installing an inexpensive watering system, such as leaking hose. This gently seeps water along the length of the beds, and can be placed on top of the soil or shallowly under it. Water is delivered directly to the plants' roots, and it can be used in conjunction with a timer for even greater efficiency. Water butts placed around the garden or advantageously near guttering and downpipes will catch rainwater from the house or greenhouse (but avoid using rainwater on young seedlings, as it can cause fungal disease).

To preserve water supplies, water only when necessary. Wilting plants are a sure sign that the bed needs watering, but if you're not sure whether your plants are short of water, poke a finger right into the soil: if it feels moist it probably doesn't need water that day. If you happen to be away on holiday during a drought, ask a friend to help out or just ignore it and face the consequences. Most established trees and hedging will not turn up their toes even when we've enjoyed weeks of dry weather.

Weeding

Weeds always grow as the irksome companions of cultivated plants, making weeding a necessary task: weeds rob garden plants of light, water and nutrients. Remove annual weeds before they have time to flower and set seed. Dig up perennial weeds such as nettles, removing roots carefully: even small pieces of root left in the soil can grow into new plants.

Weedkillers aren't discerning. They will kill desirable garden plants as well as weeds and may leave residues in the soil. Healthy soil leads to healthy plant growth; if you can do without weedkillers, your garden will be a better place.

LEFT Use a water butt to catch rainwater

ABOVE Cut out leaves that have reverted to their original, plain green, colouring

Deadheading

Deadheading is the removal of spent flowers, either to encourage a second flowering or to keep the plant looking tidy. Flowers produce seed once they have faded, so deadheading prevents seed production, effectively duping the plants into concentrating their energy on new growth (and more flowers for some) instead of directing it into producing seed.

Pinch off the dead flower heads with your fingers or snip them off with secateurs. If plants have a profusion of tiny flowers, it may be easier to trim off the faded flowers all at once with shears.

Leave some flowers if you want to collect seed from a particular plant or if you want them to self-seed around the garden. Where plants have attractive seed heads, leave these alone as well.

Pruning

Shrubs Evergreen hedges need regular trimming (which is a form of pruning) but, as a general rule, evergreen shrubs only need light pruning to keep them in shape and limit their size, and to cut out dead, diseased or damaged wood (the three Ds).

Trim hedges throughout the growing season to keep them neat and tidy. Start in spring after frosts have passed and then trim again when necessary. Hollies will probably only need one summer cut, whereas box, privet, Portuguese laurel, yew and cypress may need two or three trimming sessions. Don't prune any evergreen hedging after early autumn.

Evergreen shrubs need occasional pruning, to maintain their shape and to curtail any stems that are growing beyond their allocated space or becoming crowded. Wait until all frost risk has passed before pruning in mid-spring. Prune flowering shrubs after flowering is over: if you prune spring-flowering shrubs too early, you will cut off the developing flower buds and miss the flowers for the year.

If you prune box plants too late in autumn, the leaves may catch the sudden cold weather, turn orange and die back a little. Never mind. Give them a good dose of fertiliser come spring and they will soon recover (but try to prune a bit earlier next time).

Shrubs with variegated leaves have a natural tendency to revert to their plain deep green leaf colouring; pick off any leaves that are solidly green to keep the variegated colouring stable.

Feed or mulch your shrubs after pruning, using well-rotted manure, general-purpose fertiliser or blood, fish and bone.

Trees Evergreen trees rarely need pruning, except for the removal of dead, diseased and damaged branches in late summer.

Some old, neglected plants respond well to hard pruning in May, cutting them back to 15–30cm/6–12in above ground level. These include berberis, box, choisya, euonymus, holly and yew. If you have an overlarge or misshapen example of one of these, don't be afraid to prune it hard. However, the majority of evergreen trees and shrubs (including cypress, magnolia, rosemary and lavender)

won't stand for this and will never re-grow from the points of savage pruning.

Climbers Most climbers don't need much pruning. If you need to curb unwanted spread or maintain a good shape, it is safest to set about it before new growth starts in the middle of spring or leave it until after their spring flowering.

TOPIARY

Topiary makes smart, architectural, focal or accent points in the garden. Trees and shrubs that have dense, bushy foliage with smaller leaves – box, yew, privet and holly, for example – are clipped into sculptural shapes, such as balls, cones and pyramids, or may be fashioned into a menagerie of animals.

Small gardens and patios often rely on container-grown topiary to provide year-round green structure; in large gardens, topiary can be grown in open ground. Mature topiary plants are costly, so try to look after them well (see container planting box on page 102, for maintenance of topiary grown in pots).

Shaping your own topiary Instead of buying mature topiary, you can start with an immature plant and train it yourself, at much less expense. You will need to purchase a small plant or take cuttings from existing plants, and buy a pair of topiary or box shears.

When buying a young plant, look for healthy foliage and roots, and evenly spaced branches in the case of young trees. Most evergreen plants grow more quickly than you imagine, though holly is notoriously slow; many ivies tend to toddle in the first year, walk in the next and gallop away in their third year. It is important that your chosen tree or shrub has a good amount of growth each year, as much of this will be cut back. An annual organic mulch or application of fertiliser will encourage strong healthy growth.

Start with a small, single bushy plant (about 30cm/12in tall) and choose a shape: a square, ball, chicken or heart, for example. Then simply apply a technique called 'clip and grow', steadily and patiently sculpting the foliage through the years until the topiary reaches the desired density and size. You will need to clip once or twice a year, between April and June.

If you are growing something into a pyramid or cone

shape, leave the leader (the vertical central pointed stem tip) intact until the plant has reached the desired height. While allowing the leader to grow vertically upward, trim back the side growth each year. When forming a pyramid, you are aiming for a triangular shape, so let the bottom branches grow wider than the top stems.

To grow the plant into a ball, simply clip it into a round shape (it will probably end up the size of a tennis ball to start with). Snip out the central leader to encourage the ball to grow in width as well as height. Over the years, the tennis ball will gradually reach the size of a football and then a large beach ball, but it will not grow as vigorously as it would had the leader been left in place. The process will take some ten years and there are no shortcuts unless you buy mature topiary from a specialist nursery. This is why topiary is expensive – a lot of maintenance goes into the growing before the nurseryman can see a profit.

The new topiary will not look that impressive in the first three years, but as you clip the side shoots and let them grow out only to clip them again, the growth becomes thicker and bushier, helping to form the final shape or framework. The clipping is part of the enjoyment of topiarising trees and shrubs, and it should be done slowly and exactly, so you end up with a balanced plant. It's immensely soothing, relaxing and creative.

If you aren't feeling confident or lack a steady hand, try growing the plant through a wire frame (which you can buy in various shapes) and clipping back to it. This leaves less room for error. Place the frame over a small plant and let it grow to fill the mesh. Once foliage starts coming through the mesh, clip as above. Remove the frame once the plant grows too big for it, and continue shaping by hand.

ABOVE Box (*Buxus sempervirens*) topiary in the form of a pyramid (left) and using a wire frame in the shape of a squirrel to train the plant (right)

Hardiness

The majority of evergreen perennials, trees and shrubs are fully hardy and don't need extra protection in winter, so we need only concern ourselves with the following ratings (which follow the RHS hardiness zones).

Fully hardy: hardy to -15°C/5°F This term describes plants that are tough enough to withstand a lowest winter temperature of -15°C/5°F without lasting detriment. Plants in this category originate from cold climates and are adept at coping with cold, winds and frosts.

Frost hardy: hardy to -5°C/23°F Plants in this category can withstand temperatures as low as -5°C/23°F, but once the temperature dips below this, especially for any length of time, the plant may suffer lasting harm or death. Protect with horticultural fleece (available from garden centres) or provide shelter, such as a greenhouse or cold frame, to prevent roots being frozen or top-growth being seriously damaged by frosts. A good many frost-hardy semi-evergreen plants can lose some or all of their leaves when temperatures fall below this.

Borderline Despite being rated as fully or frost hardy, some plants may still need protection in winter, especially in cold or exposed areas. Put them in a sheltered spot, cover with a dry mulch or wrap with horticultural fleece or bubblewrap.

Problems

Every garden falls prey to pests or diseases sometimes, but evergreen perennials, trees and shrubs suffer far less from these problems than other plants.

Leaf and stem pests

Pests usually leave obvious signs of damage, from leaves munched at the edges or with holes in the centre to silky webbing or slime trails. Most infestations are very easily dealt with. Vigilance will help prevent the majority of pest attacks and plant ailments. Keep a watchful eye on your plants and you will spot problems before they get out of hand and develop into something altogether more serious.

HOUSEHOLD REMEDIES

There are some old-fashioned solutions to pests and diseases. A couple of drops of washing-up liquid added to 5 litres/1 gallon of water is an effective treatment for aphids; it has no detrimental effect on plants, so you can spray as often as you like. Add 50ml/3 tbsp of apple cider vinegar to 5 litres/1 gallon of water and spray on plant leaves to help prevent mildew and leaf spot, or spray with neem oil fortnightly if your plants are vulnerable to *Botrytis*, all mildews and rust.

Most households have these ingredients tucked in a kitchen cupboard somewhere and they are cheap and effective ways of managing your garden plant problems.

BELOW Damage caused by bay suckers (left) and an adult leafhopper (right). Vigilance is the best defence against sapsuckers and other pests

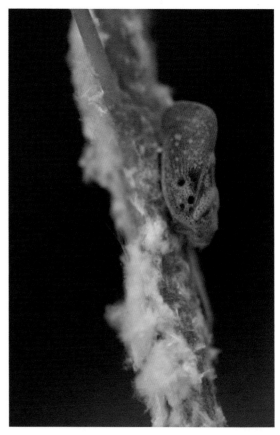

LEAF AND STEM PESTS

Aphids are a group of pests such as blackfly, greenfly and whitefly (including rhododendron whitefly), about 3mm/⅛in long, with transparent green, black or white bodies. They suck the sap from young shoots, causing curled or distorted leaves and stems and damaging new emerging growth. They usually occur in large numbers.

Spray as often as needed with a washing-up liquid solution. Encourage beneficial wildlife (the natural enemies of aphids and other pests) into the garden by planting berry-producing evergreens, which will provide shelter and food for birds and overwintering ladybirds, and nectar-filled plants such as evergreen lavenders, hellebores and geraniums. Alternatively, use a proprietary insecticide.

Bay suckers are hopping, sap-sucking green-tannish lice, about 2mm/⅛in long, that overwinter in tree bark. They lay eggs on leaf undersides and feed on the foliage in summer, causing yellowing and distortion. Although not deadly, the damage is unsightly and can spread rapidly.

Cut out affected leaves and stems, and burn them or dispose of in the household waste. If you wish, spray the remaining leaves with a proprietary insecticide.

Brown scale see **Scale insects**

Caterpillars are visible to the naked eye and may also leave silky webbing or holes in plant leaves.

Remove by hand. For a large infestation on a few leaves, remove the leaves and destroy them. Alternatively, chemical controls are available.

Earwigs are familiar brown insects, just under 2cm/¾in long, with noticeable pincers at the rear. They nibble the young leaf growth and flowers of ornamental plants, but also do a lot of good, preying on smaller insects and their eggs.

Stuff old flowerpots with straw and place them upside down on canes, to lure earwigs away from vulnerable plants; empty them daily. Alternatively, spray serious infestations with a proprietary insecticide.

Eelworms are microscopic nematodes that inhabit the stems and leaves of alpines and perennials. Symptoms include stunted, distorted stems and yellowing leaves. Plants may fail to flower.

Dig up and burn or otherwise dispose of affected plants (but do not add to the compost heap). There are no chemical or biological controls available.

Flea beetles are shiny, metallic blue-black beetles, about 3mm/⅛in long, that hop away as you approach. They mainly affect members of the brassica family, making small holes in the surface of leaves and eating seedlings. Entire plants can be destroyed.

They hibernate in plant matter over winter, so clear up all fallen leaves and rotting stems in autumn. Use sticky yellow card traps in the greenhouse in spring to catch the jumping insects. Alternatively, spray with a proprietary insecticide.

Froghoppers are pale brown sap-sucking bugs, about 6mm/¼in long, and are responsible for the white froth called cuckoo spit that appears on plant stems and leaves in summer. Tiny yellow-green nymphs hide in the spit. Adults and nymphs cause minimal damage.

Cuckoo spit is unsightly but harmless: ignore it or wash off the froth with washing-up liquid solution. Alternatively, spray with a proprietary pesticide.

Leafhoppers are sap-sucking green insects, some 3mm/⅛in long, which cause discoloured, unsightly mottling on leaves of plants such as rhododendrons.

Spread Vaseline on a piece of card and brush insects from the foliage while holding the card underneath. Alternatively, use a proprietary insecticide.

Leaf miners are the larvae of small black flies that tunnel into leaves, leaving unsightly squiggly light brown patches on the leaf surface. Damage is negligible.

Remove affected leaves and burn them, or dispose of in the household waste. If you wish, use a proprietary insecticide after removing the leaves.

Mealybugs are tiny pinkish grey sapsuckers, about 6mm/¼in long, covered in a woolly, waxy coating which makes them difficult to dislodge, and are found on greenhouse or conservatory pot plants. Their activity weakens plants and they excrete honeydew which attracts sooty mould and secondary infections.

Spray the affected plant with a washing-up liquid solution. The fatty acid in the liquid will dissolve the protective wax coating. Do this as often as necessary. Alternatively, use a proprietary insecticide.

Red spider mite is a minute green sap-feeding mite, hardly visible to the naked eye, that is most prevalent on indoor plants; it can also affect conifers and outdoor plants. It leaves silky webs around the young leaves and tips of plants; conifers may appear scorched and plant leaves become mottled, often turning bronze/brown.

Spray the underside of leaves with an upturned hose from the start of the growing period, to prevent colonisation. Hose the greenhouse daily to keep humidity levels high. Biological controls such as *Phytoseiulus persimilis* are successful if introduced into the greenhouse early in the growing season. Red spider mites are very resistant to chemical treatments.

Rhododendron whitefly see **Aphids**

Scale insects (including brown scale) are tiny sap-sucking insects that live under a protective shell (or scale) and are found on the stems and leaf undersides of woody ornamental or coniferous plants. Telltale signs are rounded brown scales with yellow centres, and plants may grow very poorly.

Be vigilant, as large infestations can be hard to treat. Apply methylated spirits to the affected areas, using cotton wool or a cotton bud. Alternatively, spray with a proprietary insecticide in early summer.

Slugs and snails are amongst the most common garden pests. They have an unquenchable appetite for leaf and flower material, particularly seedlings and lush young foliage. Look out for slime trails and leaf damage: top leaf damage signals snails while lower leaf damage is likely to be caused by slugs.

Fill a small plastic dish with beer or sugar water and place it shallowly in the soil at the base of a plant; slugs and snails are attracted by the sugary liquid and drown. Alternatively, sprinkle slug pellets sparingly around the base of plants. Biological controls are available.

Tortrix moth caterpillars are small brown-grey or green caterpillars, about 2cm/¾in long, that feed on foliage, making unsightly holes or skeletal leaves, before binding themselves inside rolled-up leaves to lay their eggs.

Pick off rolled-up leaves and dispose of them, caterpillars and all. Chemical sprays are often ineffective as the caterpillars are protected inside the leaves.

Viburnum beetles are grey-brown beetles, about 6mm/¼in long. In late spring, their eggs hatch into cream larvae with black markings which chew holes in leaves until only skeletal veins remain. Adults add to the damage in summer.

Look out for early signs of damage and remove affected foliage or prune out any stems or shoot tips covered in eggs. Lure foraging birds in to eat the larvae by hanging slices of bread or fat balls in the foliage. Alternatively, use a proprietary insecticide.

Vine weevil commonly affect plants grown in pots, but can also damage plants growing in open ground, including shrubs. The female adult beetle (easily recognised by its long pointed head) eats foliage, leaving notches along leaf edges, but it is the creamy coloured larvae, about 1 cm/⅜in long, that do most damage, feeding on plant roots. The first signs of the larvae may be yellowing leaves, poor growth or a wilting plant that does not respond to watering, but plants often collapse and die with little warning.

A nematode is available, in the form of a parasitic microscopic eelworm that enters the larvae and releases bacteria that kill the grubs; the nematodes keep reproducing inside the dead grub. Alternatively, water pots with a chemical drench.

Plant diseases

It can be difficult to spot plant diseases but, happily, few evergreen plants suffer from serious ailments. Although most plants can fall foul of complaints, these rarely prove fatal and are easily treated with early action. Warning symptoms might be poor growth or dull or discoloured leaves, for example.

Some fungal diseases are spread by airborne spores which you can do little about, but many can be prevented by good garden practice. Dirty garden tools can spread fungal bacteria: always use clean, sharp tools when pruning, and disinfect them after pruning infected material, to prevent the infection being transferred to other plants. In my experience, there is no need to seal pruning wounds as long as you have made a clean cut with no ragged ends.

Burn all infected material if possible, or dispose of it in the household waste, but do not put contaminated material on the compost heap: this will only spread it through the garden. Fungal spores and bacteria can overwinter in fallen leaves and dead twigs, so clear these up.

Improving the health of plants will make them less susceptible to disease. Feed and water plants regularly, to help them build resistance to disease, and try to water plants at soil level or use a leaky hose. Mulch plants with organic matter in spring, to aid their vigour and prevent the roots drying out.

Growing plants in overcrowded, humid conditions can leave them vulnerable to fungal attacks. To maintain a healthy airflow, avoid spacing them too closely together when planting.

Organic and non-organic fungicidal sprays are available from garden centres, but these tend to limit damage rather than eliminate the danger completely.

BELOW Hellebore suffering from leaf spot

PLANT DISEASES

***Botrytis* (grey mould)** affects weak plants and flourishes in damp conditions where air circulation is poor. It can also enter plants through wounds. Shrubs and trees are generally less severely affected than perennials. Grey, fluffy mould containing spores is clearly evident; if handled carelessly, spores will disperse in the air.

It is spread through the air, making it difficult to control, but good growing conditions and plant hygiene do much to prevent it. Remove all affected parts of the plant, cutting back to healthy growth. Burn infected material; do not add to the compost heap. There are no chemical controls available to the home gardener.

Box blight is a potentially serious fungal disease caused by damp, humid conditions. Leaves die back and affected areas are grey or brown. If not treated, part or all of the plant can die.

Water plants at the base and avoid splashing leaves. Cut plants back to increase air circulation; in serious cases, cut back radically. Burn all prunings. There are no chemical controls available to the home gardener.

Bud blast is a fungal disease that affects rhododendrons, and is further spread by leafhopper infestations. The flower buds turn sooty brown and fail to open.

Remove all affected buds and burn, to prevent the spores spreading, and treat leafhoppers on first sighting (see page 109).

Clematis wilt is a fungal disease that mainly affects large-flowered clematis. Leaves wilt and brown, and stems blacken. It rarely affects healthy plants.

Cut the plant back to where the wilt started and water with a copper-based fungicide. Plant clematis deeply to help avoid this malady.

Clubroot is a soil-borne fungal infection that attacks the roots of members of the brassica family. Symptoms include wilting leaves and yellowing, stunted growth. Affected plants have swollen, club-like roots.

It is almost impossible to control as spores remain in the ground for years. Remove and burn all affected plants; do not plant susceptible plants in the same place. When growing plants from seed, use fresh, sterilised compost and well-scrubbed pots. A drench or dip is now available.

Coral spot is a fungal disease that affects broadleaf trees and shrubs. Woody parts of the plant are covered in orange blisters and die back. It thrives on dead wood (such as log piles and fallen branches).

Cut back affected stems or branches to uninfected wood at least 15–20cm/6–8in beyond an outbreak. Disinfect tools and burn infected prunings immediately. Clear away all garden debris regularly. Fungicidal sprays are available.

Downy mildew is a fungal disease that is less common than powdery mildew. Leaves develop brown and yellow blotches, with fine white growth on the undersides. If left untreated, the plant may die.

Remove any affected leaves immediately, water at the base of plants rather than overhead, thin leaves to improve air circulation and avoid spacing plants too closely together. Fungicidal sprays are available.

Fireblight is a bacterial infection affecting any plant in the *Rosaceae* family, such as pyracantha and cotoneaster. Leaves shrivel and flowers blacken and wither, leaving the shrub looking as if it is fire damaged. If left untreated, weeping cankers form on the branches.

Prune out affected branches or stems, cutting back into healthy, non-diseased wood by about 60cm/24in. Disinfect tools and burn all infected prunings. If the plant is too far gone, dig it up and burn it. There are no chemical controls available to the home gardener.

Honey fungus is a serious fungal disease, affecting the roots of trees, shrubs and climbers. First signs may be poor growth; later, honey-coloured toadstools may appear at the base of the plant. Black bootlace threads or whitish fungal threads can be seen under the bark at the base of the plant. You are likely to lose the plant.

Dig up and burn the infected plant immediately, including as much root as possible. In small areas, dig out the affected soil to a depth of 90cm/3ft, to further limit the spread. Fill in the hole with fresh compost. Replant with plants that are less vulnerable to the disease. There are no chemical controls available to the home gardener.

Leaf spot is caused by bacteria or fungi and affects many plants, including perennials and shrubs. Brown patches appear on the leaves and gradually spread.

Remove affected leaves immediately and burn them. Thin leaves to improve air circulation. There are no chemical controls available to the home gardener.

Petal blight is a fungal disease that can affect the flowers of plants such as rhododendrons. Brown spots on the petals spread and ruin the flowers. It is often caused by wet and muggy conditions.

Remove affected flowers and flower buds, including those that have fallen to the ground, and burn them. Spray with a recommended fungicide in late spring or as soon as buds begin to colour.

***Phytophthora* root rot** see **Root rots**

Powdery mildew is a common fungal disease caused by lack of air circulation. A white powdery substance is deposited on the leaves, which turn brown if left untreated and become stunted or distorted.

Remove all affected parts of the plant. Water plants regularly. Improve air circulation by thinning leaves; avoid planting too closely together. Proprietary fungicidal sprays are available, but prevention is always better than cure.

Pyracantha scab is a serious fungal disease affecting pyracantha. Leaves may have khaki-coloured or grey spots, fruit blacken, stems die back and flowers shrivel. Excessive wet weather can exacerbate the problem.

Prune out all affected areas, including shoots, stems, flowers and fruit, and burn them. Spray with a proprietary fungicide after pruning out infected material.

Root rots (including *Phytophthora* root rot) are soil- or water-borne fungi and spores affecting woody trees and shrubs. Roots grow poorly, blacken and become brittle, and leaves discolour and die back. Rots can spread rapidly through the plant until it collapses and dies. The condition is exacerbated by poor drainage.

There is no treatment. Dig up rotting plants and burn them; don't add contaminated material to compost heaps. Replace the soil with fresh compost. To help prevent rots, always clear up garden debris, increase ventilation to the plant and improve drainage. Plant at the same depth as the pot, not too deeply.

Rust is a fungal disease affecting ornamental trees, shrubs and perennials, particularly in moist, damp conditions. Patches of orangey brown blisters develop on the undersides of leaves. If rust is left unchecked, the plant can die.

Good hygiene is the surest way to limit rust. Remove infected leaves from the plant and pick up all fallen leaves before they decompose and spread the infection; burn infected material if possible.

Silver leaf is a fungal disease affecting trees and shrubs. Leaves and branches develop a silvery grey sheen; if not caught early, branches may die. Symptoms can be slow to show: to test for infection, cut off a branch and look for internal brown staining. Wetting the cut will highlight the staining.

Prune out all infected wood, cutting along the branch until staining disappears, and burn the prunings. Mulch trees and shrubs with organic matter at their base in spring, to improve disease resistance. There are no chemical controls available to the home gardener.

Sooty mould is a black fungus that grows on the sticky honeydew excreted by aphids and other sapsuckers. It is unsightly but relatively harmless. However, when it covers large amounts of leaf surface it cuts out light, impairing the plant's growth and health.

Wash leaves (if practical) with a solution of washing-up liquid, using a clean rag, and then hose them clean. This removes the fungus and the sapsuckers, preventing honeydew. Alternatively, use a proprietary insecticide and/or fungicide.

White blister is a fungal disease that affects members of the brassica family. White circular fungal clusters appear on the undersides of leaves, resulting in stunted or distorted plant growth.

Remove all affected parts of the plant and burn them. Space plants further apart to improve air circulation and help prevent an attack. There are no chemical controls available to the home gardener.

Propagation

Raising new plants is not difficult, and can be done at almost no cost. The main ways to propagate plants are by division, growing from seed or taking cuttings.

Dividing perennials

Division is one of the easiest ways to multiply plants, and it takes very little skill to get good results first time. For evergreen perennials, division is normally carried out in spring but it can also be done in autumn, when the soil is still warm; this encourages plants to develop new roots before the onset of winter. Some of the smaller shrubs, such as lavender and vinca, can also be divided in early winter.

Choose a large clump and dig it up, roots and all. Prise the rootball apart, using two garden forks back to back (you can also use a cleaver or billhook, or even a sharp spade, to cut through the roots). If the clump is very large, repeat this process to make a number of smaller clumps, all with visible root systems, using a sharp knife to cut through tough,

DIVISION OF RHIZOMES

To divide a plant that has tuberous or rhizomatous roots, dig it up and shake the soil from the roots so you can see what you are doing. Prise the rhizomes apart by hand. Identify new young rhizomes, which will be smaller, firmer and whiter than the tough, sinewy, older ones, and pull these away from the old clump. Ensure each new rhizome has some young roots and leaves. Trim the leaves and roots by a third with a sharp, clean knife and dust with a fungicide. Replant in the final flowering position at soil level on clay soils or slightly below in sandier soils, or grow on in pots.

fibrous roots. For a smaller clump, use a kitchen knife or tease the roots apart by hand.

Replant sections taken from the outer edges of a clump and discard the older pieces at the centre, as these won't make such vigorous new plants. Plant out the divided segments in their final positions straightaway if they are large enough, or grow them on in individual pots of compost until they are ready to transplant. Keep them well watered while they re-establish.

BELOW You may need a sharp spade to divide phormiums

Growing plants from seed

Perennials, shrubs and trees can all be grown from seed. The seed-sowing process is much the same for all of them. However, the length of time needed to grow a mature plant varies greatly. A perennial plant of worthwhile size can be produced from seed within a year, but it may be years before a woody shrub or tree is a usable size, so faster methods, such as taking cuttings, are often used for shrubs and trees.

Growing evergreen plants from seed starts in autumn or spring. Many need the protection of a frost-free environment and these are sown in trays or pots and placed in an unheated greenhouse, cold frame, porch or draught-free windowsill. Some benefit from a spell in a heated greenhouse or propagator, either because they are difficult

ABOVE *Libertia grandiflora* self-seeds easily

to germinate or because this accelerates the germination process. Seeds of some plants are able to withstand winter cold so can be sown in situ, straight into their final positions. And many plants self-seed so freely that there is no need to sow them at all.

Sowing seed

Sowing times for individual plants are given in their profiles, or will be found on the seed packet if you are using bought seed. To get started, you will need:

- clean pots or seed trays
- fresh potting compost
- watering can with a rose head
- plant labels and pencil

COLLECTING SEED

You can buy seed from specialist seed suppliers, or you can collect it from plants in the garden. This is free, and is an efficient and satisfying way of raising new plants from old favourites for next to nothing (but remember that seed taken from hybrid plants is unlikely to come true: the shape, colour and flowers of the new plant may vary from those of the plant from which the seed was taken).

Always collect seed from healthy plants. Collect it in summer and autumn, when the flowers are over, and wait until the seed heads are brown, dry and brittle, as the seed inside will then be ripe, and ready for sowing. If the seed heads are still green in the autumn, bring them inside to dry out, where they will go on ripening, before storing the seed; they will rot with the onset of winter if left outside.

Crack open the dry seed cases or rub them between your fingers to release the seed inside over a piece of newspaper. Separate the chaff from the seed and either sow immediately, if the profile indicates you need to sow ripe seed, or store the seed in small, brown paper envelopes (not plastic bags, as this will make them rot). Label, date and seal the envelopes, and store in an airtight container until the appropriate sowing time.

PROTECTED GROWING

Cold frames are used to give a good start to seed that can be sown outdoors, and are a smaller and cheaper alternative to an unheated greenhouse. Simply sow seed into pots and place inside the cold frame.

They are also infinitely useful for hardening off seedlings sown in a greenhouse, helping them to acclimatise to outdoor temperatures gradually: transfer the seedlings to the cold frame and leave it open in daylight hours but closed at night. If a cold snap is forecast, tuck some fleece round the edges of the cold frame for extra insulation.

Heated propagators are mini plastic greenhouses with an electrically heated base that provides a constant, warm, protected growing environment for seedlings. They are also used for cuttings. Summer cuttings rarely need a heated propagator, but cuttings taken in autumn benefit hugely and root more quickly. A heated propagator is a good investment even if you only take a few cuttings a year, as it gives speedy results. A basic model – which is all you need – is not expensive.

Fill the pots or seed trays with unused compost to about 6mm/¼in below the rim and press it down firmly. Water lightly; if you are sowing in a greenhouse, a light drench of Cheshunt compound watered over the compost before sowing can help prevent 'damping off' (a fungal condition that kills off young seedlings grown under cover).

Sow three or four seeds to each pot or a single seed per pot, depending on the size of the seed, the space you have available and your plant needs, and cover with a thin layer of compost. If the seed is small and fine, sprinkle it thinly on top of a seed tray or surface sow in pots and cover with a dusting of compost (using a soil sieve helps ensure even coverage).

Label the pots or trays with the date sown and the name of the plant, to avoid getting the seedlings mixed up. Seeds for most of the plants in this book are placed in a cold frame or unheated greenhouse for protection. Plants that need a little encouragement to germinate are placed in a heated propagator, which provides reliable bottom heat. Water regularly with a watering can with a rose fitting, to avoid washing the seeds into puddles, and keep the soil moist but not waterlogged; whatever you do, don't let it dry out. Wait for the seeds to germinate.

Caring for seedlings

Once your seedlings appear, water them regularly, continuing to use a rose head on the watering can. Seedlings are very fragile at this stage, and need gentle handling. If the seeds were sown in a heated propagator, open the propagator vents once the seedlings have sprouted.

The seedlings will become overcrowded as they grow, competing for nutrients and space. At this point they need potting up separately, to allow them room to develop. This is known as 'pricking out'. Select the healthiest seedlings and gently ease them out of the compost using a pencil. Pick them up by the leaves, never the stem: they can grow new leaves but not a new stem if it is damaged when being handled. Pot them up individually in fresh compost, firming each seedling gently into its pot with your finger or the end of a pencil. Water regularly. (If you have sown one seed per pot, just leave them to grow on in the original pot.)

For hardier plants, sown into pots in a cold frame, wait until your seedlings have four good seed leaves and either pot them into separate containers to grow them on into larger plants, or harden them off over a three-week period before planting them out in the ground.

Young plants are more prone to slug and snail attacks than mature plants: I grow my plants to a reasonable size before planting them into their final spaces in late spring or early summer. This makes them less vulnerable to attacks from slugs and snails, but unfortunately doesn't make them impervious to them.

Hardening off

Plants that have been grown in protected conditions need a period of hardening off to get them used to the colder conditions outside before they are planted into the ground. This is done by gradually exposing the new plants to outdoor conditions over a period of weeks, once the danger of frosts has passed.

For plants grown in traditional cold frames, prop the frame open for a few hours in the daytime, closing it again at night. Leave it open for longer in the second week, and remove the lid entirely in week three. The new polycarbonate frames have plastic

you can roll up to allow fresh airflow during the day. In a greenhouse, open the vents in the daytime for a few hours and close them at night. Or if you are growing on a windowsill or in a porch, open a window or door for a few hours each day. After about three weeks, the new plants should be tough enough to move into their final growing places.

If you are using a heated propagator, wait until all seeds have germinated and then turn the heat down or off completely. Once the seedlings are big enough to handle, prick them out as usual and keep them in a frost-free place. They will need hardening off over a period of weeks before they are ready to plant out.

....

BELOW A cold frame will protect your seedlings from frosts

Growing plants from cuttings

Most perennials, shrubs and trees are easy to propagate from cuttings. This is handy if your perennials aren't large enough to divide or are not easy to grow from seed. Plants also grow to a useful size more quickly from cuttings than from seed.

A cutting is a small piece of stem or root, cut from an existing plant and grown on in a separate pot to produce a new plant, exactly like the one from which it was taken. It is important to take cuttings at the right time of year. For example, softwood cuttings will not be successful if taken in winter, because the cold will prevent new growth and kill the cutting. By contrast, hardwood cuttings root most successfully in winter, when plants are dormant.

Always take cutting material from robust, healthy-looking stems or roots on vigorous plants that are disease, pest and flower free, and use a clean, sharp knife or secateurs to take and prepare the cutting. All cuttings need a well-drained compost mixture, and must have sufficient daylight.

Softwood cuttings are taken from spring to early summer. It is best to take cuttings in the morning, when plants are more full of water: this will help avoid wilting. You can put them in the fridge until you are ready to pot them up, but it is advisable to use them immediately.

Take a cutting about 10cm/4in long from the tip of a strong, non-flowering shoot, cutting just below a leaf joint (or node), and then remove the lower leaves, leaving the top two leaves and a bare stem. (All plants have nodes, which is the part of the stem where a shoot, leaf or branch will grow. They look like small dark 'eyes' on the side of the stem.)

Dip the bottom, cut end into hormone rooting powder and tap off any excess. Insert the cutting into a pot of fresh compost mixed with a little sharp sand. (You can put two or three cuttings in each pot if space is an issue.) Firm the bases in gently with your fingertips and water well.

Label the pots and place them somewhere light and warm (in a heated propagator, on a warm windowsill or in a greenhouse), or put a clear plastic bag over the top of each pot, held with a rubber band, and then place in a warm spot, out of direct sunlight. Keep the compost moist, but not wet. Cuttings of perennials should root within six weeks. If you grow your cuttings indoors, they will need a period of hardening off before they are ready to plant out.

Basal stem cuttings are taken from the strong new shoots that emerge at the base of the plant in spring. Clear the soil away from the plant, to expose the new basal stems, which are whitish at the bottom. A new shoot will have fresh green top-growth, but the bottom will be white, turning slightly woody brown at the base where it joins the parent plant, either at ground level or slightly below. This is ideal cutting material.

With a sharp clean knife, cut the new shoot from the base of the plant so that a bit of the old woody plant material is still attached (on some plants you may have to cut slightly below the soil surface to achieve this). Trim off any damaged or uneven, ragged pieces at the base of the cutting and reduce the number of leaves to a maximum of two or three. Cuttings should be about 8cm/3in long.

Gently but firmly, push the cuttings into fresh well-drained compost to half their length. Label and keep them in a warm spot, but not in direct sunlight. The cuttings should root within eight weeks.

ABOVE Taking semi-ripe cuttings from a wall-grown *Garrya elliptica*

Greenwood cuttings are taken from early to mid-summer, from plants between the softwood and semi-ripe stages, when growth is just starting to firm up. They are carried out in exactly the same way as softwood cuttings (opposite), but are less likely to wilt. An ideal length for greenwood cuttings is 7–12cm/2¾–4½in.

Semi-ripe cuttings are taken from late summer to mid-autumn, and are suitable for shrubs and evergreen climbers. At this time of year, the stems of shrubby plants will have soft tips while being slightly harder at the bottom. Select longer leaf stems than you actually need, to allow for trimming. Place them in a plastic bag with a drop of water in it while collecting, and keep them out of the sun.

When you have collected enough material, trim the cuttings down, making a cut just below a leaf node to leave a cutting between 5cm/2in and 15cm/6in long. Then take off the lower leaves, to leave a stem with two or four leaves on top (I usually leave just two). If the leaves are large, cut them in half, to reduce water loss. Pot up as for softwood cuttings.

HEELED CUTTINGS

Select the cutting material as usual, according to whether you want a softwood or semi-ripe cutting, for example, but instead of clipping the cutting material cleanly away from the parent plant with secateurs or a knife, gently tear it away from the main stem by hand. When you pull a shoot away from the stem, it detaches from the mature plant with a sliver or 'heel' of woody material. This heel contains growth hormones that give the cutting a better chance of rooting. Heeled cuttings are particularly useful when taking cuttings from an old shrub, which will not propagate easily by other methods.

Semi-ripe cuttings are less likely to wilt than softwood cuttings, but they will take longer to root. You can put them outside in a cold frame, but they probably won't root there until spring the following year.

Internodal semi-ripe cuttings are the same as semi-ripe cuttings, except that you make the cut between two nodes instead of cutting once beneath a node, ending up with several cuttings with a short stem and one or two leaves attached. The main benefit is that you can get more cuttings per stem.

Hardwood cuttings are taken from late autumn to mid-winter, when plants are dormant and the stem wood has hardened. They are amongst the easiest and most successful methods of increasing evergreen and deciduous shrubs.

Choose a healthy stem, about 30cm/12in long, near the base of the shrub. Make sure it has at least three buds on it, and the wood is mature. Using a sharp garden knife or secateurs, cut this stem from the plant.

Hold the cutting the right way up (buds facing upwards) and make a clean, sloping cut just above the top bud and a flat straight cut below the bottom bud. You will be left with a cutting about 15cm/6in long, with a bud (with the sloping cut above it) at the top, a middle bud and bottom bud. Repeat this process with additional stems until you have the number of cuttings you require.

Tie a small batch loosely together with a piece of twine and insert the blunt ends into a pot filled with a mixture of sand, gravel and compost, or pot up single cuttings in individual pots. Alternatively, scrape a slit trench with a trowel, about 5cm/2in deep, and push single or multiple cuttings down into the earth; ensure they are not touching and bury them about half their length; firm the soil back around their bases.

Label the cuttings clearly and leave them in peace until the following autumn, when they will have rooted and be ready to plant out in the garden or to pot up separately, growing them on until they are large enough to plant out in their final positions.

Root cuttings are taken when the plant is dormant in winter, from healthy, vigorous, young roots. They are normally used for plants that produce suckers or shoots from the root area.

Choose a root about 10cm/4in long and about as thick as a pencil. Make cuts along the length of the root, depending on how many cuttings you require, so that each section is about 4cm/1½in long. Make flat cuts at the tops (the crown end) of the cuttings and angled cuts across the bottoms (the root end), so that you know which end is which (it is important that each cutting is planted the same way up as it was on the plant). Push the angled ends into well-drained fresh compost, with the flat ends flush with the soil level. Cover the root cuttings with a thin layer of sharp sand, water and label.

Rhizome root cuttings are taken in winter. Dig up the plant to reveal the fleshy whitish rhizomes, which will be smooth with bumps or 'eyes' (live buds) on them and may have white straggly roots. Wash off any soil and cut away old, tatty leaves. Use only plump healthy rhizomes, discarding brown or withered ones.

Cut each rhizome into 8cm/3in sections (trim the roots back gently to about 8cm/3in if they are very long), making sure each piece has eyes and leaves. Replant straightaway in a frost-free shady, well-drained spot, or lay them on the surface of a tray filled with fresh compost in a sheltered place until they grow roots and shoots.

PROPAGATING SUCKERING PLANTS

It is easy to get new plants from shrubs that spread by suckers. Trace the growth of a sucker from the parent plant until you find a smaller, suckering plant. Dig round the plant with a spade, trying to lift as much root as possible. Either pot it up to grow on or replant it immediately, watering thoroughly.

Rhizome root cuttings normally produce new shoots (top-growth) within three weeks, whereas the new roots may take as long as ten weeks to grow. Check that new roots have formed before potting up plantlets individually.

Layering

Many climbing plants and shrubs have pliable, flexible stems and naturally produce new plants when a stem grows along the ground and roots independently of the main plant. They will propagate successfully from layering, which is really straightforward.

In autumn or spring, find a non-flowering trailing lower stem still attached to the main plant. Remove several leaves so that the middle section is clear of leaves. Where a leaf node joins the stem, make one slanting cut through the underside of the stem, without severing it completely. Bend this section into a U shape and force the bottom of it into a hole in the soil, leaving the end of the stem sticking out. Peg the cut side of stem to the ground and cover the section lightly with soil or compost; new roots will grow at the cut. Push a bamboo cane into the soil and gently tie the leafy upright section of the stem to the cane, without disturbing the bare stem section which you have pegged down.

Keep the stem section moist through the growing season with regular watering and by autumn it will have formed its own roots. Simply detach it from the parent plant, dig it up and replant it or grow it on in a pot, watering regularly.

BELOW Layering rhododendron: make a slanting cut in the stem

The gardening year

Spring

Early spring is a great time to plant evergreens of all kinds. If you want to increase the number of plants, division is very successful at this time of year.

Plants such as the fast-growing privet may need a haircut by late spring, so sharpen your shears and keep on top of hedge trimming. And tidy up the garden, removing tatty leaves and dead or diseased growth.

Greenfly, blackfly, slugs, snails and the inevitable spring weeds are all thriving now, so be vigilant and try to keep them under control. It is time to mulch your beds, so check whether the compost is ready to use.

Summer

Container-grown plants are vulnerable to drying out in hot spells, so arrange for someone to water them if you are away.

Deadhead flowering plants, and take lavender cuttings now, while you think of it. Late summer is the last opportunity to trim any evergreen hedging before the cold and frosts set in.

Autumn

This is the ideal time to plant bare-rooted trees and shrubs, including hedging material. Do all the groundwork in advance and you will only have to water them thoroughly and plant when they arrive.

Continue taking semi-ripe cuttings from holly, magnolia and mahonia. If your garden is short of autumn colour, plant some autumn-flowering perennials for next year. Or choose shrubs and trees that have interesting berries or seed heads. Foraging birds will add a charming dimension to the garden.

ABOVE AND OPPOSITE The vivid red berries of Christmas box (*Sarcococca ruscifolia* var. *chinensis*) and frosted seed heads of *Phlomis fruticosa* ensure interest and colour through the colder months

This is the perfect time to wash pots, clean out the greenhouse or potting shed and ensure a hygienic environment for overwintering plants. Sharpen and oil your tools in readiness for the next season.

Winter

There are still a few things to sort out before you put your feet up. Provide extra insulation for plants that are vulnerable to the cold and frosts of winter, with fleece, bubblewrap or sacking, and tie in any straggling stems of climbers. Check your trellis is secure: fierce winds can pull down unstable climbing plants.

A bonfire is a great way to get rid of diseased plants. Celebrate the end of the year by enjoying a drink with friends huddled around the warmth of the fire. Cook jacket potatoes and chestnuts wrapped in foil in the ashes and feel thankful for all the delights your garden has provided.

Evergreens for specific purposes

Evergreen plants are going to be on show all year, every year, so take your time making the right choices. Even a small complement of ever-greenery in your garden will add a subtle texture that can underpin and enhance your existing planting.

Architectural

Anemanthele lessoniana
  (formerly Stipa
  arundinacea)
Cordyline 'Red Star'
Cortaderia selloana 'Pumila'
Eriobotrya japonica
Eryngium pandanifolium
Euphorbia characias subsp.
  wulfenii
E. mellifera
Fabiana imbricata f. violacea
Festuca glauca 'Elijah Blue'
Helictotrichon sempervirens
  'Saphirsprudel'
Itea ilicifolia
Juniperus procumbens 'Bonin
  Isles'
Kniphofia uvaria
Magnolia grandiflora 'Samuel
  Sommer'
Mahonia lomariifolia
Phillyrea latifolia
Phlomis fruticosa
Phormium 'Yellow Wave'
Pleioblastus viridistriatus
Polystichum munitum
P. setiferum
Yucca gloriosa

Topiary

Bupleurum fruticosum
Buxus sempervirens
Ilex aquifolium 'Argentea
  Marginata'
I.a. 'Golden van Tol'
Laurus nobilis
Osmanthus delavayi
Phillyrea latifolia
Prunus lusitanica
Santolina pinnata subsp.
  neapolitana

Hedging

Abelia × grandiflora
Atriplex halimus
Aucuba japonica

'Crotonifolia'
Berberis × stenophylla
Bupleurum fruticosum
Buxus sempervirens
Choisya ternata Sundance
Cotoneaster × watereri 'John
  Waterer'
Danae racemosa
Elaeagnus pungens 'Frederici'
Embothrium coccineum
  Lanceolatum Group
  'Ñorquinco'
Escallonia 'Apple Blossom'
Euonymus myrianthus
Gaultheria mucronata
  'Mulberry Wine'
Grevillea rosmarinifolia
Griselinia littoralis
Ilex aquifolium 'Argentea
  Marginata'
I.a. 'Golden van Tol'
Laurus nobilis
Lavandula angustifolia
  'Hidcote'
Ligustrum japonicum
  'Rotundifolium'
Lonicera nitida 'Baggesen's
  Gold'
Nandina domestica 'Fire
  Power'
Olearia paniculata
Osmanthus delavayi
Phillyrea latifolia
Photinia × fraseri 'Red Robin'
Pittosporum tobira
Pleioblastus viridistriatus
Podocarpus nivalis 'Kilworth
  Cream'
Prunus lusitanica
Pyracantha 'Golden
  Charmer'
Rhamnus alaternus
Rhaphiolepis umbellata
Rhododendron yakushimanum
  'Koichiro Wada'
Rosmarinus officinalis 'Miss
  Jessopp's Upright'

Santolina pinnata subsp.
  neapolitana
Ulex europaeus
Viburnum tinus 'Eve Price'

Climbers and wall shrubs

Azara serrata
Berberidopsis corallina
Ceanothus 'Autumnal Blue'
Clematis armandii 'Snowdrift'
C. cirrhosa 'Jingle Bells'
C. napaulensis
Cotoneaster × watereri 'John
  Waterer'
Euonymus fortunei 'Silver
  Queen'
E. myrianthus
Fabiana imbricata f. violacea
Garrya elliptica
Hardenbergia violacea
Hedera colchica 'Sulphur
  Heart' (syn. 'Paddy's
  Pride')
Hypericum 'Hidcote'
Itea ilicifolia
Lapageria rosea
Laurus nobilis
Magnolia grandiflora 'Samuel
  Sommer'
Pileostegia viburnoides
Piptanthus nepalensis
Pyracantha 'Golden
  Charmer'
Rhamnus alaternus
Sophora Sun King

Ground cover

Acaena microphylla
  'Kupferteppich'
Ajuga reptans 'Burgundy
  Glow'
Andromeda polifolia
  'Compacta'
Arabis alpina subsp. caucasica
  'Schneehaube'
Arenaria montana

Armeria juniperifolia 'Bevan's
  Variety'
Asarum hartwegii
Aubrieta 'Argenteovariegata'
Bergenia 'Autumn Magic'
Blechnum spicant
Calluna vulgaris 'Annemarie'
Carex oshimensis 'Evergold'
Cassiope 'Edinburgh'
Choisya ternata Sundance
Cistus × purpureus 'Alan
  Fradd'
Daboecia cantabrica subsp.
  scotica 'Silverwells'
Danae racemosa
Dryas octopetala
Epimedium franchetii
  'Brimstone Butterfly'
Erica carnea 'Myretoun
  Ruby'
Euonymus fortunei 'Silver
  Queen'
Farfugium japonicum
  'Aureomaculatum'
Festuca glauca 'Elijah Blue'
Gaultheria mucronata
  'Mulberry Wine'
Halimium lasianthum
Hebe 'Blue Clouds'
Hedera colchica 'Sulphur
  Heart' (syn. 'Paddy's
  Pride')
Helleborous × hybridus
  Harvington double pink
Heuchera 'Persian Carpet'
Hypericum 'Hidcote'
Iberis sempervirens
Juniperus procumbens 'Bonin
  Isles'
Leucothoe fontanesiana
Liriope muscari
Luzula sylvatica 'Aurea'
Nandina domestica 'Fire
  Power'
Ophiopogon planiscapus
  'Nigrescens'
Ozothamnus rosmarinifolius

Pachysandra terminalis
Photinia × fraseri 'Red Robin'
Podocarpus nivalis 'Kilworth
  Cream'
Polygala chamaebuxus var.
  grandiflora
Polypodium cambricum
  'Richard Kayse'
Prostanthera cuneata
Rhododendron 'Azurika'
Ruscus aculeatus
Ruta graveolens 'Jackman's
  Blue'
Sagina subulata var. glabrata
  'Aurea'
Santolina pinnata subsp.
  neapolitana
Sarcococca ruscifolia var.
  chinensis
Saxifraga 'Sugar Plum Fairy'
Sedum spurium 'Schorbuser
  Blut'
Thymus serpyllum 'Pink
  Chintz'
Vinca minor 'Atropurpurea'
Waldsteinia ternata

Slopes and banks
Acaena microphylla
  'Kupferteppich'
Ajuga reptans 'Burgundy
  Glow'
Arabis alpina subsp.
  caucasica 'Schneehaube'
Arenaria montana
Armeria juniperifolia 'Bevan's
  Variety'
Asplenium scolopendrium
Aubrieta 'Argenteovariegata'
Bergenia 'Autumn Magic'
Blechnum spicant
Calluna vulgaris 'Annemarie'
Camellia japonica 'Lady Loch'
Campanula portenschlagiana
Cassinia fulvida
Cassiope 'Edinburgh'
Choisya ternata Sundance
Cistus × purpureus 'Alan
  Fradd'
Daboecia cantabrica subsp.
  scotica 'Silverwells'
Elaeagnus pungens 'Frederici'
Epimedium franchetii
  'Brimstone Butterfly'
Erica carnea 'Myretoun
  Ruby'
Euonymus fortunei 'Silver
  Queen'

Fatsia japonica
Hebe 'Blue Clouds'
Hedera colchica 'Sulphur
  Heart' (syn. 'Paddy's
  Pride')
Hypericum 'Hidcote'
Iberis sempervirens
Juniperus procumbens 'Bonin
  Isles'
Leucothoe fontanesiana
Ligustrum japonicum
  'Rotundifolium'
Nandina domestica 'Fire
  Power'
Ophiopogon planiscapus
  'Nigrescens'
Pachysandra terminalis
Photinia × fraseri 'Red Robin'
Pieris 'Forest Flame'
Podocarpus nivalis 'Kilworth
  Cream'
Rosmarinus officinalis 'Miss
  Jessopp's Upright'
Ruta graveolens 'Jackman's
  Blue'
Sagina subulata var. glabrata
  'Aurea'
Saxifraga 'Kinki Purple'
S. 'Sugar Plum Fairy'
Skimmia × confusa 'Kew
  Green'
Vinca minor 'Atropurpurea'
Waldsteinia ternata

Coastal areas
Atriplex halimus
Aucuba japonica
  'Crotonifolia'
Berberis × stenophylla
Bupleurum fruticosum
Calluna vulgaris 'Annemarie'
Cassinia fulvida
Ceanothus 'Autumnal Blue'
Choisya ternata Sundance
Erica carnea 'Myretoun
  Ruby'
Eryngium pandanifolium
Erysimum 'Bowles's Mauve'
Escallonia 'Apple Blossom'
Garrya elliptica
Griselinia littoralis
Hebe 'Blue Clouds'
Iris unguicularis
Juniperus procumbens 'Bonin
  Isles'
Laurus nobilis
Lonicera nitida 'Baggesen's
  Gold'

Magnolia grandiflora 'Samuel
  Sommer'
Myrtus communis
Olearia paniculata
Phormium 'Yellow Wave'
Phillyrea latifolia
Phlomis fruticosa
Rhamnus alaternus
Rosmarinus officinalis 'Miss
  Jessopp's Upright'
Ruscus aculeatus
Ruta graveolens 'Jackman's
  Blue'
Sophora Sun King
Teucrium fruticans 'Azureum'
Ulex europaeus
Viburnum tinus 'Eve Price'
Viola cornuta 'Icy But Spicy'
Yucca gloriosa

Boggy soil
Carex oshimensis 'Evergold'
Luzula sylvatica 'Aurea'

Woodland
Andromeda polifolia
  'Compacta'
Asarum hartwegii
Asplenium scolopendrium
Bergenia 'Autumn Magic'
Blechnum spicant
Camellia japonica
  'Lady Loch'
Carex oshimensis 'Evergold'
Cassiope 'Edinburgh'
Desfontainia spinosa
Embothrium coccineum
  Lanceolatum Group
  'Ñorquinco'
Fatsia japonica
Gaultheria mucronata
  'Mulberry Wine'
Geranium endressii
Helleborous × hybridus
  Harvington double pink
Kalmia latifolia
Leucothoe fontanesiana
Liriope muscari
Luzula sylvatica 'Aurea'
Mahonia lomariifolia
Nandina domestica 'Fire
  Power'
Osmanthus delavayi
Pachysandra terminalis
Phillyrea latifolia
Pieris 'Forest Flame'
Piptanthus nepalensis
Pittosporum tobira

Podocarpus nivalis 'Kilworth
  Cream'
Polypodium cambricum
  'Richard Kayse'
Polystichum munitum
P. setiferum
Pyracantha 'Golden
  Charmer'
Rhododendron
  yakushimanum 'Koichiro
  Wada'
Ruscus aculeatus
Sagina subulata var. glabrata
  'Aurea'
Sarcococca ruscifolia var.
  chinensis
Saxifraga 'Kinki Purple'
S. 'Sugar Plum Fairy'
Skimmia × confusa 'Kew
  Green'
Viola cornuta 'Icy But Spicy'
Waldsteinia ternata

Full shade
Ajuga reptans 'Burgundy
  Glow'
Asarum hartwegii
Asplenium scolopendrium
Aucuba japonica
  'Crotonifolia'
Berberis × stenophylla
Bergenia 'Autumn Magic'
Blechnum spicant
Buxus sempervirens
Camellia japonica 'Lady Loch'
Choisya ternata Sundance
Danae racemosa
Hedera colchica 'Sulphur
  Heart' (syn. 'Paddy's
  Pride')
Lapageria rosea
Liriope muscari
Lonicera nitida 'Baggesen's
  Gold'
Mahonia lomariifolia
Pileostegia viburnoides
Podocarpus nivalis 'Kilworth
  Cream'
Polygala chamaebuxus var.
  grandiflora
Polystichum munitum
P. setiferum
Ruscus aculeatus
Sarcococca ruscifolia var.
  chinensis
Skimmia × confusa 'Kew
  Green'
Viburnum tinus 'Eve Price'

Vinca minor 'Atropurpurea'

Waldsteinia ternata

North-facing aspects

Ajuga reptans 'Burgundy Glow'

Aucuba japonica 'Crotonifolia'

Camellia japonica 'Lady Loch'

Epimedium franchetii 'Brimstone Butterfly'

Kalmia latifolia

Lapageria rosea

Mahonia lomariifolia

Pileostegia viburnoides

Skimmia × confusa 'Kew Green'

Berries and decorative seed pods/heads

Berberis × stenophylla

Clematis cirrhosa 'Jingle Bells'

C. napaulensis

Cordyline 'Red Star'

Coronilla valentina subsp. glauca 'Citrina'

Cotoneaster × watereri 'John Waterer'

Danae racemosa

Daphne bholua 'Jacqueline Postill'

Dryas octopetala

Eriobotrya japonica

Euonymus fortunei 'Silver Queen'

E. myrianthus

Fabiana imbricata f. violacea

Fatsia japonica

Gaultheria mucronata 'Mulberry Wine'

Griselinia littoralis

Ilex aquifolium 'Argentea Marginata'

I.a. 'Golden van Tol'

Laurus nobilis

Libertia grandiflora

Ligustrum japonicum 'Rotundifolium'

Liriope muscari

Lonicera nitida 'Baggesen's Gold'

Mahonia lomariifolia

Myrtus communis

Nandina domestica 'Fire Power'

Ophiopogon planiscapus 'Nigrescens'

Osmanthus delavayi

Phillyrea latifolia

Photinia × fraseri 'Red Robin'

Piptanthus nepalensis

Pittosporum tobira

Podocarpus nivalis 'Kilworth Cream'

Prunus lusitanica

Pyracantha 'Golden Charmer'

Rhamnus alaternus

Rhaphiolepis umbellata

Ruscus aculeatus

Sarcococca ruscifolia var. chinensis

Viburnum tinus 'Eve Price'

Fragrant flowers/ aromatic bark and leaves

Abelia × grandiflora

Asarum hartwegii

Azara serrata

Berberis × stenophylla

Buddleja asiatica

Carpenteria californica

Cassinia fulvida

Choisya ternata Sundance

Cistus × purpureus 'Alan Fradd'

Clematis armandii 'Snowdrift'

C. cirrhosa 'Jingle Bells'

C. napaulensis

Cordyline 'Red Star'

Coronilla valentina subsp. glauca 'Citrina'

Daphne bholua 'Jacqueline Postill'

Elaeagnus pungens 'Frederici'

Erica carnea 'Myretoun Ruby'

Eriobotrya japonica

Escallonia 'Apple Blossom'

Euphorbia mellifera

Geranium endressii

Helichrysum italicum

Iris unguicularis

Itea ilicifolia

Juniperus procumbens 'Bonin Isles'

Laurus nobilis

Lavandula angustifolia 'Hidcote'

Leucothoe fontanesiana

Ligustrum japonicum 'Rotundifolium'

Lonicera nitida 'Baggesen's Gold'

Magnolia grandiflora 'Samuel Sommer'

Mahonia lomariifolia

Myrtus communis

Olearia paniculata

Osmanthus delavayi

Ozothamnus rosmarinifolius

Phillyrea latifolia

Phlomis fruticosa

Pittosporum tobira

Polygala chamaebuxus var. grandiflora

Prostanthera cuneata

Prunus lusitanica

Pyracantha 'Golden Charmer'

Rhaphiolepis umbellata

Rosmarinus officinalis 'Miss Jessopp's Upright'

Ruta graveolens 'Jackman's Blue'

Salvia officinalis 'Icterina'

Santolina pinnata subsp. neapolitana

Sarcococca ruscifolia var. chinensis

Skimmia × confusa 'Kew Green'

Teucrium fruticans 'Azureum'

Thymus serpyllum 'Pink Chintz'

Ulex europaeus

Viburnum tinus 'Eve Price'

Viola cornuta 'Icy But Spicy'

Silver-leaved

Atriplex halimus

Convolvulus cneorum

Eryngium pandanifolium

Festuca glauca 'Elijah Blue'

Helichrysum italicum

Helictotrichon sempervirens 'Saphirsprudel'

Lavandula angustifolia 'Hidcote'

Phlomis fruticosa

Ruta graveolens 'Jackman's Blue'

Santolina pinnata subsp. neapolitana

Teucrium fruticans 'Azureum'

Autumn leaf colour

Bergenia 'Autumn Magic'

Cotoneaster × watereri 'John Waterer'

Epimedium franchetii 'Brimstone Butterfly'

Euonymus myrianthus

Nandina domestica 'Fire Power'

Cream/white flowers

Abelia × grandiflora

Arabis alpina subsp. caucasica 'Schneehaube'

Arenaria montana

Atriplex halimus

Buddleja asiatica

Carpenteria californica

Cassinia fulvida

Cassiope 'Edinburgh'

Choisya ternata Sundance

Cistus × purpureus 'Alan Fradd'

Clematis armandii 'Snowdrift'

C. cirrhosa 'Jingle Bells'

C. napaulensis

Convolvulus cneorum

Cordyline 'Red Star'

Cotoneaster × watereri 'John Waterer'

Daboecia cantabrica subsp. scotica 'Silverwells'

Dryas octopetala

Elaeagnus pungens 'Frederici'

Eriobotrya japonica

Escallonia 'Apple Blossom'

Fatsia japonica

Gaultheria mucronata 'Mulberry Wine'

Iberis sempervirens

Leucothoe fontanesiana

Libertia grandiflora

Ligustrum japonicum 'Rotundifolium'

Lonicera nitida 'Baggesen's Gold'

Magnolia grandiflora 'Samuel Sommer'

Myrtus communis

Nandina domestica 'Fire Power'

Olearia paniculata

Ophiopogon planiscapus 'Nigrescens'

Osmanthus delavayi

Ozothamnus rosmarinifolius

Photinia × fraseri 'Red Robin'

Pieris 'Forest Flame'

Pileostegia viburnoides

Pittosporum tobira

Prostanthera cuneata

Prunus lusitanica

Pyracantha 'Golden Charmer'

Plant index

Picture credits

Photographs supplied by Garden World Images Ltd

Asarum hartwegii (p.13) © Cotswold Garden Flowers
Saxifraga 'Kinki Purple' (p.44) © Longhouse Plants
Magnolia grandiflora 'Samuel Sommer' (p.58) © Burncoose Nurseries

Saxifraga 'Sugar Plum Fairy' (p.63) © Cotswold Garden Flowers
Viola cornuta 'Icy But Spicy' (p.75) © Cotswold Garden Flowers
Garden centre (p.99) © Meadow Croft Garden Centre